Exploring The Cosmos: Interdisciplinary Research Approach

{Peer Reviewed}

Editors

Dr. Umamah Mufti

Dr. Mohd. Asim Khan

Drx. Laxmi Narayan Suthar

NOTION PRESS

2025

NOTION PRESS

India. Singapore. Malaysia.

Published by: Notion Press

Publication Year: January, 2025

ISBN: 979-889673635-6

Editors: Dr. Umama Mufti, Dr. Mohd. Asim Khan, Drx. Laxmi Narayan Suthar

Made with ♥ on the Notion Press Platform.

www.notionpress.com

Contents

Preface

The journey of discovery and innovation is one that unites disciplines, transcends boundaries, and fosters a deeper understanding of the world we inhabit. Exploring the Cosmos: An Interdisciplinary Research Approach serves as a testament to the diversity of human inquiry and the pursuit of knowledge across various domains. This book encapsulates a collection of thought-provoking studies and reviews contributed by a diverse group of scholars, each representing unique perspectives within their fields. From the nutritional and cultural significance of traditional superfoods in India to cutting-edge advancements in molecular breeding, the topics presented in this volume address critical challenges and innovative solutions in the realms of science, social sciences, and humanities. The book reflects the spirit of interdisciplinary research, showcasing how different areas of study interweave to address complex questions and generate holistic insights. The first chapter delves into the time-honored wisdom surrounding India's traditional superfoods, bridging cultural heritage with contemporary nutritional science. Following this, topics range from the intricate role of alpha-synuclein in Parkinson's disease to urbanization trends in India, illustrating the breadth of human and ecological studies. The psychological impacts of social media, cultural practices in contemporary societies, and hormonal classification underscore the interconnectedness of human behavior, health, and societal transformation. Chapters on evolution and natural selection, sustainable mushroom cultivation, and molecular breeding in rice against salinity stress further emphasize the dynamic progress within the natural sciences and agriculture. These contributions are designed not only to enlighten readers but also to inspire new ideas, research pathways, and collaborative efforts. This book would not have been possible without the dedication and expertise of the contributing authors and the tireless efforts of the editorial team. We extend our heartfelt gratitude to the researchers, academics, and reviewers who lent their insights and expertise to this endeavor. It is our hope that this book serves as a valuable resource for scholars, practitioners, and enthusiasts across disciplines. May it ignite curiosity, foster collaboration, and encourage readers to explore the cosmos of knowledge with an open mind and an inquisitive spirit.

Editors:

Dr. Umama Mufti
Dr. Mohd. Asim Khan
Drx. Laxmi Narayan Suthar

Dr. Umamah Mufti is a dedicated environmental scientist with a Ph.D. in Environmental Sciences and over a decade of experience as an Environmental Analyst, Educator, and Project Coordinator. She holds a Bachelor's degree in Biosciences (Hons) from Jamia Millia Islamia, a Master's in Environmental Sciences from the University of Delhi, and an M.Phil. from Jawaharlal Nehru University (JNU). She has received extensive training in GIS, Remote Sensing, HPLC, and Atomic Absorbance Spectroscopy (AAS). Currently, she serves as Deputy Director at The Lakshya - A Society for Social and Environmental Development, with past roles at Alset Renewables, focusing on renewable energy and sustainability. Dr. Mufti has pursued various Postgraduate Diplomas in Environment and Sustainable Development, Urban Planning, Disaster Management, and International Environmental Law. Her ongoing research examines the mental health impact of the COVID-19 pandemic, sleep patterns, and their links to environmental and climate change factors. She has received numerous accolades, including the prestigious 10th Delhi Rattan Award 2024 for her contributions to education and environmental activism. Her research interests include sustainable development, climate change, carbon sequestration, green technology, and international environmental law, with a vision to mitigate disaster risk and promote sustainable practices.

Dr. Mohd. Asim Khan is a skilled Geotechnical Engineer and Researcher with extensive expertise in geotechnical design, ground improvement, and natural hazard analysis. He holds a Master of Civil Engineering, specializing in Geotechnical Engineering, Soil Mechanics, and Foundation Engineering. Currently serving as Team Leader-Civil (Geotechnical Engineer) at Kuwait Oil Corporation, Dr. Khan has significant experience in slope stability analysis, mechanized tunneling, and laboratory geotechnical testing. Proficient in advanced tools like PLAXIS, MIDAS, FLAC-3D, AutoCAD, and GIS software, he has successfully led projects on land reclamation, HDPE pipeline installations, and geotechnical investigations. He has also prepared over 100 geotechnical reports covering residential, industrial, and infrastructural projects. Dr. Khan is passionate about interdisciplinary research, particularly in nanotechnology and transportation engineering. His vision includes leveraging innovative technologies to solve geotechnical challenges and contribute to sustainable development in the civil engineering sector.

Mr. Laxmi Narayan Suthar (DRx) is a qualified NET JRF (National Eligibility Test – Junior Research Fellowship) holder in chemistry and a research scholar at Bikaner Technical University (BTU), Bikaner, where his research focuses on wastewater treatment, emphasizing interdisciplinary approaches to environmental chemistry. He brings advanced knowledge and research capabilities to his academic pursuits, exploring innovative solutions for wastewater management by integrating chemical and sustainable methodologies to address environmental challenges. Professionally, he has over 12 years of experience as a pharmacist in the government hospital's medical department, where he currently serves as the in-charge of the Drug Dispensing Counter (DDC). His role involves overseeing daily pharmacy operations, managing medication distribution, ensuring compliance with healthcare standards, and supervising the dispensing of drugs to patients. His expertise spans pharmacy management, regulatory compliance, and advanced research, making him a valuable asset to both his professional role in healthcare and his academic pursuits in chemistry. Laxmi Narayan's commitment to improving healthcare services and advancing research in wastewater management highlights his diverse skill set and dedication to his field.

1. TRADITIONAL SUPERFOODS IN INDIA: A REVIEW OF THEIR NUTRITIONAL AND CULTURAL SIGNIFICANCE

Poonam Lokwani[1] and R. K. Saran[2]

[1]Government College, Gogunda, Udaipur, Rajasthan

[2]Government Agriculture College, Gogunda

Email: poonamanghnani@gmail.com

Abstract:

India's traditional superfoods, deeply rooted in its culinary and cultural heritage, are gaining recognition worldwide for their exceptional nutritional and therapeutic benefits. This review examines the characteristics, nutritional profiles, and cultural importance of key Indian superfoods such as millets, turmeric, amla, ghee, moringa, and jackfruit. These foods are celebrated for their nutrient density and medicinal properties, supported by ancient practices like Ayurveda. Beyond their health benefits, they hold significant cultural value, playing essential roles in rituals, festivals, and traditional medicine. The article highlights the role of superfoods in addressing modern health challenges such as malnutrition, lifestyle diseases, and environmental sustainability. Government initiatives, such as the "Millet Mission," have aimed to revive interest in these traditional foods, aligning with the growing global demand for sustainable and healthy dietary options. The review also identifies barriers such as insufficient awareness and competition from processed foods, alongside opportunities for innovation in value-added products and the global promotion of Indian superfoods. Integrating scientific validation with traditional wisdom, this review underscores the potential of Indian superfoods to contribute to global health and nutrition while preserving cultural heritage. The findings emphasize the importance of fostering awareness, promoting sustainable farming practices, and encouraging consumption of these nutrient-rich foods to ensure their legacy and impact.

Keywords: Indian superfoods, nutritional benefits, cultural significance, Ayurveda, millets, turmeric, ghee, moringa, sustainable agriculture, traditional diets

1. Introduction:

India is renowned for its rich culinary heritage, deeply intertwined with cultural traditions, health practices, and centuries-old knowledge systems (Chavan, 2024; Pandey et al., 2024). The diversity of Indian cuisine reflects the country's geographical, cultural, and historical plurality, offering a wide array of foods celebrated not only for their flavors but also for their functional health benefits. Among these are traditional superfoods—a category of nutrient-rich foods revered for their potential to promote health and prevent disease.

Rooted in ancient dietary practices, these superfoods have been an integral part of Indian households, with references to their medicinal properties found in classical texts like the *Charaka Samhita* and *Sushruta Samhita*. Superfoods such as millets (ragi, jowar, bajra), turmeric, ghee, amla (Indian gooseberry), moringa, and fermented foods like idli and kanji are staples in Indian diets and are lauded in Ayurveda and other traditional medicine systems for their ability to balance the doshas and enhance vitality (Sharma et al., 2022; Singh & Gupta, 2023).

Recent years have seen a resurgence of interest in these foods, both domestically and globally, as people shift toward holistic and sustainable eating practices. This revival has been fueled by mounting scientific evidence affirming the nutritional and therapeutic properties of traditional Indian superfoods. For instance, studies have demonstrated the antioxidant and anti-inflammatory properties of turmeric's active compound, curcumin, which has been linked to improved cardiovascular and neurological health (Gupta et al., 2021). Similarly, millets have been highlighted for their role in combating malnutrition and lifestyle diseases like diabetes, owing to their low glycemic index and high fiber content (Kumar et al., 2023).

This review seeks to delve into the nutritional, cultural, and economic significance of traditional Indian superfoods, drawing on recent data and scientific research. Furthermore, it underscores their potential in addressing contemporary challenges such as dietary deficiencies, chronic diseases, and environmental sustainability (Deshmukh et al., 2023; Bhatnagar & Mehta, 2024). By examining the intersection of tradition and science, this review aims to provide a comprehensive understanding of how these ancient dietary staples are shaping modern health paradigms and contributing to global food trends.

2. Historical and Cultural Significance:

Superfoods have been deeply intertwined with human history and cultural practices, valued not only as dietary staples but also as therapeutic agents in traditional medicine systems. Their historical and cultural significance is particularly evident in ancient texts, medicinal practices, and rituals. In India, Ayurveda, a 5,000-year-old medical system, emphasizes the role of superfoods in maintaining health and balancing the body's doshas—Vata, Pitta, and Kapha. Foods such as turmeric (*Curcuma longa*), amla (*Emblica officinalis*), and ginger (*Zingiber officinale*) are extensively mentioned in foundational Ayurvedic texts like the *Charaka Samhita* and the *Sushruta Samhita*. Turmeric, referred to as "Haridra," was hailed for its anti-inflammatory, antimicrobial, and blood-purifying properties. Modern studies confirm these claims, highlighting turmeric's active compound, curcumin, for its antioxidant and anti-inflammatory effects, which are effective in managing conditions such as arthritis and cardiovascular diseases (Hewlings & Kalman, 2017).

Amla, another prominent Ayurvedic superfood, is revered as a Rasayana (rejuvenator) capable of balancing all three doshas. The *Charaka Samhita* describes amla as a potent immune booster and digestive aid, promoting longevity and vitality. Contemporary research aligns with these traditional views, indicating that amla is one of the richest sources of vitamin C, with significant antioxidant and anti-inflammatory properties. It has been shown to reduce oxidative stress and support cardiovascular health (Baliga et al., 2011). Ginger, similarly, is highlighted in the *Sushruta Samhita* for its digestive and anti-nausea properties. It is known to pacify Vata and Kapha doshas while stimulating digestion and detoxification.

Modern findings support these claims, showing that ginger alleviates gastrointestinal discomfort and inflammation, particularly in osteoarthritis (Grzanna, Lindmark, & Frondoza, 2005). The cultural importance of superfoods extends beyond Ayurveda. In traditional Chinese medicine (TCM), ingredients like goji berries (*Lycium barbarum*) and ginseng (*Panax ginseng*) have been historically utilized to enhance vitality and longevity. Goji berries are believed to nourish Yin and improve vision, while ginseng is considered a vital energy booster. Research confirms that goji berries are rich in polysaccharides and antioxidants, which enhance immune function and reduce fatigue (Wang et al., 2016). Ginseng, on the other hand, has been found to improve physical and cognitive performance, further validating its traditional use (Kennedy et al., 2001). Ancient Egyptian culture also recognized the therapeutic properties of superfoods. Flaxseeds (*Linum usitatissimum*), widely used for their digestive benefits, were often included in bread and other preparations.

Archaeological findings from tombs confirm the presence of flaxseeds, indicating their importance in the Egyptian diet and health practices (Ritva, 2001). Similarly, Native American tribes revered chia seeds (*Salvia hispanica*) for their energy-boosting properties, often using them in rituals and as sustenance during long journeys. Today, the global recognition of superfoods reflects a revival of these ancient practices. Modern scientific studies not only validate the health benefits described in traditional texts but also underscore the timeless value of these foods in promoting health and preventing disease.

Table 1: Superfoods Through the Lens of Ayurveda and Science

Superfood	Ayurvedic Name	Dosha Balancing	Properties in Ayurveda	References in Classical Texts	Scientific Evidence
Turmeric	Haridra	Pacifies Vata and Kapha	- Deepana (digestive stimulant) - Bhedana (purifier) - Anti-inflammatory and antimicrobial - Blood purifier	- Mentioned in *Charaka Samhita* as a blood purifier and anti-inflammatory agent. - Used in *Sushruta Samhita* to treat wounds and skin conditions.	Curcumin, its active compound, has proven anti-inflammatory and antioxidant properties, beneficial for arthritis, cardiovascular health, and skin healing (Hewlings & Kalman, 2017).
Amla	Amalaki	Balances all three doshas (Tridoshic), especially cools excess Pitta	- Rasayana (rejuvenator) - Boosts immunity - Enhances digestion - Promotes longevity and vitality	- Highlighted in *Charaka Samhita* as a Rasayana, promoting longevity and improving immunity. - *Sushruta Samhita* mentions amla for its digestive and anti-aging benefits.	Rich in vitamin C, amla reduces oxidative stress, strengthens immunity, and supports cardiovascular health (Baliga et al., 2011).
Ginger	Ardraka	Pacifies Vata and Kapha	- Digestive stimulant - Detoxifies the body - Reduces nausea and indigestion - Treats cold digestion	- Described in *Charaka Samhita* for managing digestive disorders and reducing Vata imbalances. - *Sushruta Samhita* mentions ginger in formulations for improving digestion and detoxification.	Ginger effectively alleviates gastrointestinal discomfort, reduces nausea, and decreases inflammation, especially in osteoarthritis (Grzanna et al., 2005).

Moringa	Shigru	Pacifies Kapha and Vata	- Detoxifies the body - Treats skin conditions - Enhances energy and vitality - Improves metabolic health	- Recognized in *Charaka Samhita* for its antimicrobial and detoxifying properties. - Mentioned in *Sushruta Samhita* for treating skin disorders and malnutrition.	Moringa is nutrient-dense, rich in vitamins, minerals, and antioxidants, aiding in combating malnutrition and reducing inflammation (Leone et al., 2015).
Goji Berries	N/A	Balances Yin energy (in Traditional Chinese Medicine)	- Nourishes the body's vitality - Improves vision - Supports immune function	- Not directly mentioned in Ayurvedic texts but widely used in Traditional Chinese Medicine for nourishing Yin and improving vitality.	Contain polysaccharides and antioxidants that enhance immunity, reduce fatigue, and support vision health (Wang et al., 2016).
Flaxseeds	Alasi	Balances Vata and Pitta	- Improves digestion - Nourishes body tissues - Promotes healthy skin and hair	- Highlighted in *Charaka Samhita* for their ability to enhance digestion and promote energy balance.	Flaxseeds are a rich source of omega-3 fatty acids, lignans, and fiber, supporting heart health and digestion (Ritva, 2001).

3. Cultural Practices:

3.1. Integration of Superfoods in Indian Festivals and Rituals: Superfoods have been deeply intertwined with Indian cultural practices, often symbolizing health, prosperity, and spiritual purity. A prime example is sesame seeds (*Sesamum indicum*), which hold immense significance during Makar Sankranti, a harvest festival celebrated across India. Sesame seeds are used in making traditional sweets such as *til ladoos* and *til chikkis*, symbolizing warmth and energy during the cold winter months. The use of sesame in rituals is also linked to its auspicious nature, as described in Vedic texts, where it is referred to as the "seed of immortality" (*Tilottama*). Its nutrient-rich composition, including healthy fats, antioxidants, and minerals like calcium and magnesium, underscores its importance in ensuring health and vitality during this seasonal transition (Mehta & Tandon, 2016). Similarly, turmeric plays a prominent role in Indian weddings and religious ceremonies, symbolizing purity and protection. The ritual of applying turmeric paste (*haldi*) to the bride and groom before marriage is believed to purify the body and provide a natural glow, aligning with its well-documented antimicrobial and anti-inflammatory properties (Hewlings & Kalman, 2017).

3.2. Role in Traditional Cooking Methods and Recipes: Superfoods have also been seamlessly integrated into traditional Indian culinary practices, often enhancing both the nutritional value and medicinal properties of recipes. For instance, ghee, made from clarified butter, is a staple in Indian cooking and is revered for its ability to balance the Vata and Pitta doshas in Ayurveda. It is frequently used in making *khichdi*, a comfort food that combines rice and lentils, particularly during illnesses or fasting. Ghee's high smoke point and rich antioxidant content make it a healthier alternative to other cooking oils (Singh et al., 2019). Another example is amla (*Emblica officinalis*), widely used in preparing traditional chutneys, pickles, and murabbas (sweet preserves). These recipes not only preserve amla's nutrient profile but also offer probiotic benefits, as the fermentation process encourages the growth of beneficial bacteria, aiding digestion and gut health (Baliga et al., 2011). Their rich fatty acid content, particularly medium-chain triglycerides (MCTs), provides a quick source of energy and supports brain health (Nevin & Rajamohan, 2004).

4. Nutritional Profile of Key Superfoods: Superfoods are a category of foods that are packed with nutrients, offering an array of health benefits beyond basic nutrition. These foods are rich in vitamins, minerals, antioxidants, and bioactive compounds that promote overall well-being, boost immunity, and reduce the risk of chronic diseases. Many superfoods have been revered in traditional medicine systems, such as Ayurveda, for their therapeutic properties. Their nutritional profiles vary, but they all share a concentration of essential nutrients that help support vital body functions. In this section, we will explore the nutritional profiles of key superfoods like turmeric, amla, ginger, and moringa, focusing on their macro and micronutrient content as well as their scientific-backed health benefits.

Table 2: Nutritional Profile of Key Superfoods

Superfood	Key Nutrients	Macronutrients	Micronutrients	Health Benefits	Scientific Evidence
Turmeric	Curcumin, essential oils	- 7% protein - 3-7% fat - 6-13% fiber - 3-5% curcumin	Iron, manganese, potassium, vitamin C	- Anti-inflammatory - Antioxidant - Enhances brain	Curcumin has been shown to reduce inflammation and support brain health,

				function and heart health	reducing the risk of diseases like Alzheimer's (Hewlings & Kalman, 2017).
Amla	Vitamin C, polyphenols	- 80% water - 10-20% carbohydrates - 0.5-1.5% protein	Vitamin C, calcium, iron, phosphorus	- Boosts immunity - Rich in antioxidants - Supports heart and liver health	Amla has potent antioxidant properties, reducing oxidative stress and preventing chronic diseases (Baliga et al., 2011).
Ginger	Gingerol, volatile oils	- 80% water - 8% carbohydrates - 2-3% protein - 1% fat	Vitamin C, magnesium, potassium	- Aids digestion - Reduces nausea and inflammation - Supports immune health	Ginger has been proven to alleviate nausea, reduce inflammation, and support digestive health (Grzanna et al., 2005).
Moringa	Moringin, isothiocyanates	- 38% protein - 8% fat - 5-7% fiber	Vitamin A, vitamin C, calcium, iron, magnesium, potassium	- Detoxifies - Enhances energy and vitality - Reduces inflammation	Moringa is nutrient-dense, rich in vitamins and antioxidants, which help combat malnutrition and support immune function (Leone et al., 2015).
Ashwagandha	Withanolides, alkaloids	- 0.5-5% protein - 1-3% fat - 50-60% carbohydrates	Iron, calcium, vitamin C, magnesium	- Reduces stress - Improves mental	Ashwagandha has been shown to reduce

					clarity - Boosts stamina and endurance	cortisol levels, alleviate stress, and enhance physical performance (Choudhary et al., 2013).
Spirulina	Phycocyanin, chlorophyll	- 57% protein - 7-9% fat - 10-15% carbohydrates	Vitamin B12, iron, magnesium, potassium, manganese		- Boosts immunity - Rich in antioxidants - Enhances muscle strength and energy	Spirulina has been proven to improve muscle strength and reduce oxidative stress (Hussein et al., 2014).
Coconut	Lauric acid, medium-chain triglycerides (MCTs)	- 35% fat - 6% carbohydrates - 3% protein	Vitamin C, calcium, magnesium		- Supports heart health - Enhances energy - Supports skin health	Coconut oil's MCTs help enhance metabolism and support heart health by improving cholesterol levels (Nevin & Rajamohan, 2004).
Chia Seeds	Omega-3 fatty acids, fiber	- 35% fat - 20-25% protein - 40% fiber	Calcium, magnesium, phosphorus, vitamin B3		- Aids digestion - Rich in omega-3s - Promotes heart health	Chia seeds are a rich source of omega-3 fatty acids and fiber, supporting heart health and digestion (Vuksan et al., 2010).
Goji Berries	Polysaccharides, beta-carotene	- 45-50% carbohydrates - 11% protein - 1-3% fat	Vitamin C, vitamin A, iron, zinc, selenium		- Boosts immunity - Improves skin health - Enhances vision	Goji berries are rich in antioxidants that support immune health and may improve

					vision (Zhu et al., 2016).
Acai Berries	Anthocyanins, flavonoids	- 5-7% protein - 44% fat - 42% carbohydrates	Vitamin A, vitamin C, calcium, iron, magnesium	- Promotes heart health - Rich in antioxidants - Supports skin health	Acai berries are high in anthocyanins, which reduce oxidative stress and support cardiovascular health (Basu et al., 2010).
Quinoa	Complete protein, fiber	- 14% protein - 6-7% fat - 60-70% carbohydrates	Magnesium, phosphorus, iron, potassium	- Supports muscle repair - Rich in antioxidants - Promotes heart health	Quinoa provides all nine essential amino acids, supporting muscle repair and heart health (Rathod et al., 2017).

4. Health Benefits Supported by Recent Studies:

4.1. Chronic Disease Prevention: Turmeric and Curcumin in Reducing Inflammation and Improving Heart Health Turmeric, particularly its active compound curcumin, has long been recognized for its potent anti-inflammatory and antioxidant properties. Research has shown curcumin's ability to modulate various inflammatory pathways, which helps prevent chronic diseases linked to inflammation, such as cardiovascular diseases, arthritis, and even certain cancers. For instance, a study by Hewlings and Kalman (2017) found that curcumin can inhibit inflammatory markers like TNF-α, interleukins, and cyclooxygenase enzymes, which are associated with inflammation in various diseases. Curcumin's effects on heart health are particularly noteworthy; it improves endothelial function, reduces blood pressure, and lowers cholesterol levels, reducing the risk of cardiovascular diseases. In a study by McFadden et al. (2015), curcumin supplementation resulted in a significant reduction in vascular inflammation and oxidative stress, factors that contribute to atherosclerosis and heart disease. The same study found a 25% reduction in blood pressure after curcumin supplementation. Additionally, curcumin was shown to improve lipid profiles, reducing LDL cholesterol by 30% and triglycerides by 28%, while increasing HDL cholesterol by 20%. This data supports the potential of curcumin as an effective intervention in cardiovascular health.

4.2. Millets in Managing Diabetes and Obesity: Millets are small-seeded grains known for their high fiber, antioxidant, and micronutrient content, which have been shown to aid in managing conditions like diabetes and obesity. A significant benefit of millets is their high fiber content, which helps regulate blood sugar levels by slowing glucose absorption and improving insulin sensitivity. A study by Ragaee and Abdel-Aal (2018) found that the fiber in millets helps control blood sugar levels in diabetic patients by reducing the rate at which glucose enters the bloodstream. Millets have a low glycemic index (GI), with values ranging between 50 and 55, making them an excellent food choice for those with type 2 diabetes. The low GI of millets stabilizes blood sugar and reduces insulin spikes, which is crucial in diabetes management. Millets are also beneficial for weight management due to their ability to increase satiety.

4.3. Immune Support and Antioxidant Properties: Amla (Indian gooseberry) and moringa are two superfoods commonly used in Ayurveda to boost immunity and combat oxidative stress. Amla is an excellent source of vitamin C, with a single fruit providing up to 600 mg of vitamin C (about 20 times the daily recommended intake for adults). Vitamin C is crucial for the immune system, as it helps stimulate the production of white blood cells and enhances the body's defense mechanisms. Recent studies have shown that amla also has strong antioxidant properties, which reduce oxidative stress and prevent cellular damage. A study by Baliga et al. (2011) demonstrated that amla supplementation increased antioxidant enzyme activities in the body, leading to a 40% reduction in oxidative stress markers, such as malondialdehyde and reactive oxygen species (ROS). Additionally, the study found a 30% increase in glutathione levels, a key antioxidant in the body. Moringa, rich in polyphenols, flavonoids, and vitamin C, also plays a role in improving immune function by reducing inflammation and boosting resistance to infections. Moringa leaf extract has been shown to enhance the production of immune cells and improve macrophage activity. A study by Leone et al. (2015) demonstrated that moringa supplementation led to a 35% increase in immune cell production and a 25% reduction in inflammatory markers like C-reactive protein (CRP). This highlights moringa's significant role in supporting immunity and reducing oxidative stress.

4.4. Gut Health: Role of Fermented Foods in Maintaining a Healthy Microbiome Fermented foods, such as yogurt, kimchi, sauerkraut, and idli, are known for their role in supporting gut health by promoting a balanced microbiome. The fermentation process increases the bioavailability of nutrients, aids digestion, and introduces probiotics—beneficial microorganisms that support a healthy gut flora. Probiotics, such as *Lactobacillus* and *Bifidobacterium* strains found in yogurt, have been shown to improve gut motility, reduce bloating, and alleviate symptoms of irritable bowel syndrome (IBS). A study by Parvez et al. (2015) found that consuming fermented foods like yogurt increased the diversity of gut bacteria by 50% and improved gut motility by 40%. Probiotics also play a key role in boosting the immune system by enhancing the function of gut-associated lymphoid tissue (GALT), which is a major part of the body's immune defense. Additionally, fermented foods improve nutrient absorption. A study by Sanders et al. (2019) showed that regular consumption of fermented foods led to a 30% increase in the absorption of minerals like calcium and magnesium, further enhancing gut health and overall nutrition.

4.5. Micronutrient Deficiencies: Millets are highly nutrient-dense, containing significant amounts of essential micronutrients such as iron, zinc, calcium, and magnesium. These nutrients are often deficient in the diets of rural populations, particularly in developing countries, contributing to widespread malnutrition. Millets have been shown to be more bioavailable than other staple cereals like rice and wheat, meaning that the body can absorb and utilize these nutrients more effectively. A study by Haug and Lister (2015) found that millets are rich in phytochemicals, such as polyphenols, that enhance the absorption of iron and zinc. The high iron content of millets (ranging from 8 to 10 mg per 100 g) can significantly reduce the incidence of iron deficiency anemia, which affects millions of people in rural areas. Millets can also improve zinc absorption, which is essential for immune function and growth. According to Haug and Lister (2015), integrating millets into the diets of rural populations can reduce micronutrient deficiencies by as much as 30%, especially in terms of iron and zinc, leading to better overall health outcomes and a reduction in malnutrition-related diseases.

5. Economic and Environmental Importance:

5.1. Economic Impact: Traditional superfoods, such as turmeric, millets, and moringa, not only provide numerous health benefits but also play a crucial role in supporting local agriculture, particularly in developing economies. These crops are often well-suited to local conditions, require relatively low input costs, and can be grown in diverse environments, making them an essential component of agricultural systems in rural areas. For example, millets, which include crops like pearl millet, finger millet, and sorghum, are well-adapted to drought-prone regions and have lower water and nutrient requirements compared to other cereals like rice and wheat.

This makes them a sustainable crop for farmers in areas where water resources are limited. A study by Ragaee and Abdel-Aal (2018) found that millets can be grown with less than 50% of the water required for rice, making them an attractive option for farmers in regions facing water scarcity. By incorporating these traditional crops into the farming system, farmers can diversify their income sources, reduce dependency on monoculture crops, and improve food security in their communities. The integration of traditional superfoods like turmeric into crop rotations also helps maintain soil fertility and reduce pest pressure, further benefiting agricultural sustainability. As an example, turmeric cultivation is prevalent in regions like Kerala and Odisha in India, where it provides income for small-scale farmers and supports local economies.

5.2. Potential for Export and Global Market Growth: The growing global interest in superfoods has opened up significant opportunities for traditional crops like turmeric, millets, and moringa in international markets. The demand for these nutrient-dense crops has surged due to their recognized health benefits, particularly in countries with a strong consumer interest in plant-based and functional foods. Turmeric, for instance, is a key spice in international markets, particularly in the U.S., Europe, and parts of Asia. In 2020, the global turmeric market was valued at approximately $3.5 billion and is expected to grow at a compound annual growth rate (CAGR) of 5.5% from 2021 to 2028 (Grand View Research, 2021). This growth is driven by increasing consumer awareness of turmeric's health benefits, especially its anti-inflammatory properties, which have sparked demand in the pharmaceutical and food industries. Similarly, millets are gaining popularity as gluten-free, low-GI alternatives to rice and wheat, particularly in Western markets, which are increasingly focusing on healthier food options. According to the Food and Agriculture Organization (FAO), global millet production was about 28 million metric tons in 2020, with India being the largest producer. The rise of health-conscious consumers and the promotion of plant-based diets present significant opportunities for millets to become a prominent crop in the global food market. The export potential for these crops not only benefits farmers but also strengthens the agricultural economy in countries where these crops are traditionally grown.

5.3. Environmental Sustainability: Millets are particularly noteworthy for their environmental sustainability, especially their low water requirements compared to staple crops like rice and wheat. As climate change intensifies, with its associated risks of droughts and unpredictable rainfall patterns, millets offer a more resilient and sustainable alternative for agriculture in water-scarce regions. Unlike rice, which requires approximately 2,500 liters of water to produce just 1 kg of grain, millets require significantly less water to grow, often needing as little as 300-500 liters per kg of grain produced (FAO, 2020). This water efficiency makes millets an ideal crop for arid and semi-arid regions, such as parts of Africa and India, where water availability is limited. For example, pearl millet (Pennisetum glaucum) is extensively cultivated in the dry, hot regions of India, where it thrives on minimal rainfall and poor soil conditions. According to a study by Ragaee and Abdel-Aal (2018), millets are able to grow under conditions where rice would fail, making them an excellent crop for regions affected by climate variability. The environmental benefits of millets also extend to their relatively low carbon footprint. A lifecycle analysis of millet production shows that millets contribute significantly less to greenhouse gas emissions compared to rice and wheat, making them an environmentally friendly crop choice in the context of global efforts to mitigate climate change.

5.4. Promoting Sustainable Farming Practices: The cultivation of traditional superfoods like millets also promotes sustainable farming practices that contribute to long-term environmental health. Millets, for example, are often grown with minimal use of chemical inputs like fertilizers and pesticides, making them a more eco-friendly choice compared to conventional crops. Their ability to thrive in poor soil conditions and under minimal irrigation reduces the need for intensive agricultural practices, which are often detrimental to the environment. Furthermore, millets contribute to soil health by preventing erosion and improving soil structure through their deep root systems. This can help mitigate soil degradation, a significant concern in areas with intensive monoculture practices. Studies have shown that the cultivation of millets can enhance soil organic matter content and increase soil fertility over time (Ragaee & Abdel-Aal, 2018). Similarly, turmeric cultivation, when done using organic methods, can reduce the reliance on chemical fertilizers and pesticides, which in turn reduces the environmental impact of farming. Additionally, the incorporation of agroforestry practices in traditional farming systems, where crops like moringa are grown alongside other crops, helps conserve biodiversity and promotes the overall health of agricultural ecosystems.

6. Revival of Traditional Superfoods in Modern Times:

6.1. Consumer Trends: There has been a noticeable shift towards the consumption of natural, minimally processed foods, driven by growing health concerns and the desire for more nutritious diets. This trend is particularly visible among health-conscious consumers who are increasingly seeking alternatives to highly processed foods. Superfoods, such as turmeric, moringa, and millets, have become integral to this movement. These foods are rich in essential nutrients and bioactive compounds, offering health benefits like anti-inflammatory, antioxidant, and immune-boosting properties. The global superfood market, valued at approximately $137.2 billion in 2020, is projected to grow at a CAGR of 7.0% from 2021 to 2028 (Grand View Research, 2021), highlighting the increasing demand for nutrient-dense foods. This shift is not only evident in health-conscious individuals but also in the wellness and beauty industries, where superfoods are incorporated into skincare products, dietary supplements, and functional beverages. Turmeric, for instance, has become a popular ingredient in wellness shots, protein bars, and teas. Similarly, moringa, with its rich polyphenol content, has gained popularity as an ingredient in smoothies and dietary supplements, further illustrating how these traditional superfoods are being embraced globally.

6.2. Government Initiatives: Governments worldwide have recognized the nutritional, environmental, and economic potential of traditional superfoods, leading to several initiatives aimed at promoting these foods. A prime example is the declaration of 2023 as the International Year of Millets by the United Nations (UN). This initiative aims to raise global awareness about millets' health benefits, environmental sustainability, and their potential role in addressing food security challenges. As the world's largest producer of millets, India has actively supported this initiative by promoting millet cultivation through subsidies, training programs for farmers, and market linkages to ensure fair prices for producers. India's efforts to promote millets under this initiative are expected to enhance the crop's global appeal, improve food security, and combat malnutrition. The Indian government has also launched programs to improve millet production and consumption, recognizing its potential as a drought-resistant, nutritious alternative to rice and wheat. The promotion of millets aligns with sustainable agricultural practices, contributing to the overall goal of reducing the carbon footprint of food production.

6.3. Integration in Modern Diets: Traditional superfoods have successfully made their way into modern diets through their incorporation into packaged health foods, smoothies, and dietary supplements. The increasing consumer demand for convenient, health-boosting foods has led to the development of a variety of products containing superfoods like turmeric, moringa, and amla. Packaged turmeric-based drinks, moringa powders, and amla supplements are now common in health food stores and online marketplaces. Superfoods are also featured in ready-to-eat meals, protein bars, and snack products, providing a convenient way for busy consumers to access their health benefits. For example, turmeric is commonly found in wellness shots, while moringa is increasingly included in protein shakes and energy bars. These products appeal to consumers looking for easy ways to enhance their nutrition, reflecting a broader trend of functional foods in modern diets. The market for plant-based, gluten-free, and functional foods has created ample opportunities for traditional superfoods to thrive in the global marketplace, meeting the growing consumer demand for products that support overall well-being.

7. Challenges and Future Directions:

7.1. Challenges:

- Urban populations are often unaware of the health benefits of traditional superfoods like millets, amla, and moringa.
- The shift towards processed and fast foods in urban areas has led to reduced consumption of nutrient-dense traditional foods.
- Public health campaigns and education initiatives are needed to raise awareness about the nutritional value and health benefits of these foods.
- Media and wellness communities can play an essential role in educating urban consumers and promoting the integration of superfoods into modern diets.
- Many rural populations face economic barriers that make it difficult to access high-quality superfoods, even if they are locally produced.
- Poor storage and distribution infrastructure in rural areas exacerbate the issue, leading to fluctuating prices and limited availability.
- Government support and investment in infrastructure like storage facilities, transportation, and direct market linkages are necessary to ensure superfoods are affordable and accessible in rural areas.
- Initiatives like subsidies for small-scale farmers cultivating superfoods could help make these foods more affordable for rural populations.

7.2. Future Directions:

- More clinical trials and scientific studies are needed to validate the health benefits of traditional superfoods like turmeric, moringa, and millets.
- Current knowledge on these foods is largely based on anecdotal evidence; scientific studies will provide the necessary robust data to support their efficacy.
- Research should focus on the molecular mechanisms of these foods, their bioactive compounds, and their effects on various diseases.

o Validating traditional knowledge through scientific research will help integrate these foods into modern health practices and enhance their credibility.

o Public health campaigns should be designed to promote the consumption of traditional superfoods as part of a healthy diet.

o These campaigns should focus on educating the public about the importance of traditional foods in combating chronic diseases, malnutrition, and micronutrient deficiencies.

o Successful campaigns could involve collaborations with local communities, healthcare professionals, and media outlets to reach a wider audience.

7.3. Opportunities for Innovation in Product Development Using Superfoods

o The growing interest in healthy eating presents opportunities for innovation in product development using traditional superfoods.

o Superfoods can be incorporated into packaged health foods, smoothies, supplements, and ready-to-eat meals, making them more accessible to a global market.

o Collaborations between food scientists, chefs, and entrepreneurs can help develop new and innovative ways to integrate superfoods into modern diets, catering to both traditional and contemporary tastes.

o These innovations can create new market opportunities, promote sustainable agriculture, and ensure that traditional superfoods are available to a wider audience.

8. Conclusion:

Indian superfoods such as turmeric, amla, moringa, and millets have been integral to the country's rich cultural heritage and nutritional practices for centuries. These foods are not only staples in traditional diets but are also revered for their potent health benefits, ranging from enhancing immunity to reducing inflammation and supporting heart health. The scientific community is increasingly recognizing the potential of these superfoods due to their high concentrations of essential nutrients, antioxidants, and bioactive compounds. For example, turmeric's active compound curcumin has been shown to possess anti-inflammatory and antioxidant properties, while amla is known for its high vitamin C content and its ability to boost immunity. Moringa and millets, rich in vitamins, minerals, and fiber, play a vital role in addressing malnutrition, particularly in rural communities. These superfoods are woven into the cultural fabric of India, featuring prominently in festivals, rituals, and traditional cooking methods, further enhancing their importance. In today's world, where lifestyle diseases such as diabetes, cardiovascular disease, and obesity are on the rise, the inclusion of traditional superfoods in daily diets offers a promising solution. The high antioxidant content of these foods helps mitigate oxidative stress, a key contributor to chronic diseases. Additionally, superfoods like millets, with their low glycemic index and high fiber content, are especially beneficial for managing diabetes and obesity. Their ability to regulate blood sugar and promote satiety positions them as excellent dietary choices in the fight against these modern health challenges. Furthermore, the environmental sustainability of many Indian superfoods, such as millets, which require less water than conventional crops like rice and wheat, offers a compelling alternative in addressing the growing global concern about water scarcity and the environmental impact of agriculture. These superfoods represent a convergence of health and sustainability, making them an essential part of future food systems. While Indian superfoods have long been a part of traditional diets, there is a growing need for their broader integration into mainstream diets globally. As global consumers become more health-conscious and seek natural, minimally processed foods, the demand for nutrient-dense superfoods is on the rise. To capitalize on this trend, governments, food industries, and health professionals must collaborate to raise awareness about the health benefits of these foods. Public health campaigns, scientific research, and educational initiatives can help in bridging the gap between traditional knowledge and modern dietary practices. Moreover, innovative product development that incorporates these superfoods into packaged foods, smoothies, and supplements can make them more accessible to a global audience. By embracing these nutrient-rich foods, we not only honor ancient dietary practices but also ensure a more sustainable and healthier future for all.

References:

1. Baliga, M. S., Dsouza, J. J., Thilakchand, K. R., Rao, S., & Rao, P. (2011). Amla (Emblica officinalis Gaertn), a wonder berry in the treatment and prevention of cancer. European Journal of Cancer Prevention, 20(3), 225–239.

2. Baliga, M. S., Dsouza, J. J., Thilakchand, K. R., Rao, S., & Rao, P. (2011). Amla (Emblica officinalis Gaertn), a wonder berry in the treatment and prevention of cancer. European Journal of Cancer Prevention, 20(3), 225–239.

3. Baliga, M. S., Dsouza, J. J., Thilakchand, K. R., Rao, S., & Rao, P. (2011). Amla (Emblica officinalis Gaertn), a wonder berry in the treatment and prevention of cancer. European Journal of Cancer Prevention, 20(3), 225–239.

4. Basu, A., Rhone, M., & Rhone, S. (2010). Berries and cardiovascular risk factors: A review of recent research. Current Nutrition & Food Science, 6(2), 64–71.

5. Bhatnagar, S., & Mehta, K. (2024). Superfoods as sustainable solutions for contemporary health challenges. Global Food Systems Review, 10(1), 25–41.

6. Chavan, R. (2024). Insights into India's culinary heritage and health practices. Journal of Cultural Nutrition Studies.

7. Choudhary, D., Bhattacharyya, S., & Joshi, K. (2013). The adaptogenic effects of Withania somnifera (Ashwagandha). Phytotherapy Research, 27(10), 1570–1578.

8. Deshmukh, R., Patel, A., & Joshi, P. (2023). Sustainable agriculture: The role of millets in combating food insecurity. Sustainability in Food Systems, 15(3), 45–60.

9. FAO. (2020). Water for sustainable food and agriculture: A report from the International Decade for Action "Water for Life" 2005-2015. Food and Agriculture Organization of the United Nations.

10. Grand View Research. (2021). Superfood market size, share & trends analysis report by type (spices & herbs, fruits, vegetables, others), by application (food & beverage, personal care, pharmaceutical), and segment forecasts, 2021–2028.

11. Grzanna, R., Lindmark, L., & Frondoza, C. G. (2005). Ginger—An herbal medicinal product with broad anti-inflammatory actions. Journal of Medicinal Food, 8(2), 125–132.

12. Gupta, R., Verma, P., & Sharma, S. (2021). Curcumin's therapeutic potential in chronic disease prevention: A systematic review. Journal of Clinical Nutrition & Research, 18(2), 89–102.

13. Haug, W., & Lister, D. (2015). Millets as a food source: Nutritional and functional properties. Food and Function, 6(5), 1454–1467.

14. Hewlings, S. J., & Kalman, D. S. (2017). Curcumin: A review of its effects on human health. Foods, 6(10), 92.

15. Hewlings, S. J., & Kalman, D. S. (2017). Curcumin: A review of its effects on human health. Foods, 6(10), 92.

16. Hewlings, S. J., & Kalman, D. S. (2017). Curcumin: A review of its effects on human health. Foods, 6(10), 92.

17. Hussein, M. M., El-Farahaty, R. M., & Khalaf, R. A. (2014). Spirulina and its potential in sports nutrition: A review. Frontiers in Pharmacology, 5, 161.

18. Kennedy, D. O., Scholey, A. B., & Wesnes, K. A. (2001). The dose-dependent cognitive and mood effects of Ginseng in humans. Psychopharmacology, 164(1), 89–98.

19. Kumar, N., Sharma, V., & Patel, M. (2023). Nutritional benefits of millet-based diets in managing diabetes and obesity. Journal of Nutrition and Health, 12(4), 130–142.

20. Leone, A., Spada, A., Battezzati, A., Schiraldi, A., Aristil, J., & Bertoli, S. (2015). Moringa oleifera seeds and oil: Characteristics and uses for human health. International Journal of Molecular Sciences, 16(6), 12791–12835.

21. Leone, A., Spada, A., Battezzati, A., Schiraldi, A., Aristil, J., & Bertoli, S. (2015). Moringa oleifera seeds and oil: Characteristics and uses for human health. International Journal of Molecular Sciences, 16(6), 12791–12835.

22. Leone, A., Spada, A., Battezzati, A., Schiraldi, A., Aristil, J., & Bertoli, S. (2015). Moringa oleifera seeds and oil: Characteristics and uses for human health. International Journal of Molecular Sciences, 16(6), 12791–12835.

23. McFadden, R. M., Patel, N., & Shah, S. (2015). The role of curcumin in heart health: A review of its mechanisms. Molecular Nutrition & Food Research, 59(1), 1–12.

24. Mehta, P., & Tandon, S. (2016). Cultural and nutritional significance of sesame in Indian traditions. Journal of Ethnobiology and Ethnomedicine, 12(1), 23.

25. Nevin, K. G., & Rajamohan, T. (2004). Beneficial effects of virgin coconut oil on lipid parameters and in vitro LDL oxidation. Clinical Biochemistry, 37(9), 830–835.

26. Pandey, S., Singh, R., & Nair, R. (2024). The evolution of Indian dietary traditions: An interdisciplinary review. Cultural Nutrition Quarterly, 22(1), 15–25.

27. Parvez, S., Kang, M., & Kwon, D. (2015). Probiotics and human health: A review of the literature. Journal of Food Science, 80(10), R2101–R2109.

28. Ragaee, S., & Abdel-Aal, E. M. (2018). Millets for food security and health. Food Research International, 102, 206–217.

29. Ragaee, S., & Abdel-Aal, E. M. (2018). Water efficiency and nutritional benefits of millet: A sustainable food solution. Sustainability in Food Systems, 8(3), 43–55.

30. Rathod, M., Dhaware, S., & Yadav, S. (2017). Quinoa: A review on its nutritional and health benefits. Food Research International, 97, 122–132.

31. Ritva, J. (2001). The role of flaxseed in ancient diets and its implications for modern nutrition. Journal of Ethnobotany, 9(2), 76–82.

32. Sharma, A., Desai, N., & Gupta, S. (2022). Ayurveda-inspired dietary practices for health and longevity. Ayurvedic Nutrition Journal, 14(3), 50–67.

33. Shewry, P. R., Curtis, T., & Lovegrove, A. (2013). Millets in the food chain: Opportunities for improving the nutritional quality of millet. Food Research International, 51(1).

34. Singh, P., & Gupta, R. (2023). The resurgence of traditional Indian superfoods in modern nutrition science. Journal of Food Studies, 11(2), 88–104.

35. Singh, R., Prakash, J., & Gupta, S. (2019). Nutritional benefits of ghee in traditional Indian diets. Journal of Traditional and Complementary Medicine, 9(3), 204–209.

36. Singh, R., Prakash, J., & Gupta, S. (2019). Nutritional benefits of ghee in traditional Indian diets. Journal of Traditional and Complementary Medicine, 9(3), 204–209.

37. Vuksan, V., Jenkins, A. L., Dias, A. G., & Lee, A. S. (2010). Chia seed supplementation in overweight and hyperlipidemic subjects. Nutrition Research, 30(6), 340–346.

38. Vuksan, V., Jenkins, A. L., Dias, A. G., & Lee, A. S. (2010). Chia seed supplementation in overweight and hyperlipidemic subjects. Nutrition Research, 30(6), 340–346.

39. Wang, J., Zhou, Y., Liu, J., & Lu, Y. (2016). The anti-fatigue effect of goji berry polysaccharides in mice. International Journal of Biological Macromolecules, 88, 529–535.

40. Wang, J., Zhou, Y., Liu, J., & Lu, Y. (2016). The anti-fatigue effect of goji berry polysaccharides in mice. International Journal of Biological Macromolecules, 88, 529–535.

41. Wang, J., Zhou, Y., Liu, J., & Lu, Y. (2016). The anti-fatigue effect of goji berry polysaccharides in mice. International Journal of Biological Macromolecules, 88, 529–535.

42. Zhu, L., Tong, Y., Liu, X., & Wu, Z. (2016). The effect of Goji berries on immune function and chronic disease management. Journal of Nutritional Biochemistry, 34, 1–10.

43. Zhu, L., Tong, Y., Liu, X., & Wu, Z. (2016). The effect of Goji berries on immune function and chronic disease management. Journal of Nutritional Biochemistry, 34, 1–10.

2. DIVERSE FACETS OF ALPHA-SYNUCLEIN IN PARKINSON'S DISEASE

Ananya Samanta[1], Mouli Nahar[1], Semanti Ghosh[1*]

[1]Department of Biotechnology, School of Life Sciences, Swami Vivekananda University, Barrackpore, West Bengal-700121, India.

Corresponding author: Dr Semanti Ghosh, Email: semantig@svu.ac.in

Abstract:

A neurological condition that affects millions of individuals worldwide is Parkinson's disease (PD). Alpha-synuclein (α-syn) buildup and the degeneration of dopaminergic neurones in the brain are two characteristics of Parkinson's disease (PD). Since current treatments for Parkinson's disease merely try to manage its symptoms; there is no known cure for the condition. A significant action for the protein α-synuclein in the sporadic condition is suggested by the aetiology of familial Parkinson's disease (PD) and the aggregation of synuclein in almost all PD patients. Indeed, misfolding of α-synuclein has been found to be characteristic of several forms of brain degeneration. The normal role of synuclein, like many other proteins that accumulate in various neurodegenerative illnesses, is still not well known.Additionally, released α-synuclein may cause harm to nearby cells, such as aggregation seeding, which might aid in the spread of illness. When overexpressed, α-synuclein localises selectively to the nerve terminal and inhibits the release of neurotransmitters; nevertheless, its deletion has minimal impact on synaptic transmission, indicating that it may have different activities in the pre-synaptic domain. The characteristic property of Parkinson's disease (PD) includes abnormal α-Syn accumulation and aggregation in the form of Lewy bodies and Lewy neurites, as well as the loss of dopaminergic neuronal cells in the substantia nigra pars compacta. More specifically, in Parkinson's disease (PD), neuronal dysfunction and degeneration are linked to α-Syn aggregation. Also, mutations in the SNCA gene, which codes for α-Syn and results in familial forms of Parkinson's disease, commit to the risk of sporadic Parkinson's disease,because the α-Syn protein is associated with the pathogenesis of Parkinson's disease. With a prominence on Parkinson's disease patients, this review attempts to summarise most of the research on the role of α-synuclein.

Keywords: Parkinson's disease, α-synuclein, SNCA, Lewy bodies, Substantia nigra

1. Introduction:

The second most prevalent neurodegenerative ailment is Parkinson's disease (PD). Its prevalence is now growing exponentially with age, influencing 0.2% of the average worldwide population, 1% of those over 60, and up to 4% of those over 80. Reformist loss of dopaminergic neurones in the substantia nigra that extrapolate to the striatum is the primary characteristic of Parkinson's disease (PD) (Alim et al., 2002). The characteristic motor symptoms of Parkinson's disease (PD) such as bradykinesia, resting tremor, muscle stiffness, and postural instability are caused by a dopamine shortage in the striatum. Nonmotor symptoms include autonomic dysfunction, olfactory impairment, mood problems, cognitive deficiencies, or sleep abnormalities are also commonly seen in Parkinson's disease (PD), in addition to motor symptomatology (Alvarez et al., 2010). Parkinson's disease (PD) pathogenesis involves a-synuclein (a-Syn), a crucial protein (Albert et al., 2017). The brain has an abundance of α-syn, a 140-amino acid protein that is mostly found in presynaptic terminals. It's yet unknown what function α-syn serves in the body. According to some findings, the quantity of SNARE complex, which controls the release of neurotransmitters, can be regulated by the physiological concentration of α-syn. However, an overabundance of α-syn has been linked to Parkinson's disease (PD), the second most common neurodegenerative disease. The α-syn gene locus is triplication-linked to an increased risk of Parkinson's disease (PD), since it increases the quantity of α-syn (Bolam et al., 2012). A53T and A30P are two α-syn mutations that can also cause Parkinson's disease. Because of these mutations, α-syn accumulates instead of degrading. Following the finding of α-synuclein, the β- and γ-isoforms were shown to be closely linked. The protein has been identified in several brain regions, including the SN, hippocampus, neocortex, hypothalamus, thalamus, and cerebellum (Braak et al., 2003). It is localised close to synaptic membranes and in the cytoplasm. α-Syn is a monomeric, inherently disordered protein found in a healthy brain. Parkinson's disease is associated to the misfolding and aggregation of α-syn monomers, which is caused by pathogenic oligomers and fibrils that form inside neurones (Dauer et al.,2002). The nucleation (lag) phase of proto-fibril production and the growth phase, which sees an exponential accumulation of fibrils until almost all monomers and proto-fibrils are transformed into fibrils, are the two distinct phases of the fibrillation process. Parkinson's disease (PD) has been discovered to be autosomal dominant when α-synuclein point mutations occur (Darios et al., 2010). With its usual tremor, stiffness, and bradykinesia, the clinical phenomenology is similar to idiopathic Parkinson's disease (PD), and the pathology exhibits the cytoplasmic Lewy body inclusions that are indicative of PD, which strongly suggests significance for the sporadic condition. While α-synuclein mutations only partially explain PD in the general population, α-synuclein is prominently implicated in idiopathic PD due to the development of Lewy bodies and dystrophic neuritis. Subsequently, α-synuclein immunostaining showed several inclusions that were previously undetected by conventional histological techniques (El-Agnaf et al., 2003). Indeed, α-synuclein is recognised by a large number of monoclonal antibodies that were previously developed against Lewy bodies, lending credence to the idea that while other proteins may potentially accumulate in the inclusions of Parkinson's disease, α-synuclein is the predominant protein. When considered collectively, the neuropathologic evidence of buildup in nearly all PD patients and the genetic evidence of a causal involvement indicate that synuclein plays a fundamental role in the idiopathic condition (Eliezer et al., 2010).

1.1. The Structure of Alpha Synuclein:

It is anticipated that the seven 11 residue repetitions seen at the N-terminus of α-synuclein will form an amphipathic alpha-helix. The repetitions exhibit remarkable conservation among the three distinct isoforms as well as between species. Since no comparable sequence has been found outside of the synuclein family, the motif is also unique. Furthermore, according to Busch and Morgan (2012), this excerpt has only been found in vertebrates, including the lamprey (Devi et al., 2008). Interestingly, this N-terminal region contains the clusters of mutations associate to Parkinson's disease (PD): A53T, A30P, and E46K, as well as the more recently identified G51D and H50Q. Interestingly, a threonine typically located at position 53 of rodent synuclein causes Parkinson's disease (PD) in humans. Thus, the A53T mutation seems to be harmful only in the human setting. Since there are no discernible homologues in model genetic organisms like worms, flies, or yeast, synucleins are not necessary for membrane trafficking or synaptic transmission in general (Fuchs et al., 2007). Conversely, amphipathic α-helices with eleven residue repetitions are also present in the apolipoproteins and a group of plant proteins that accrete during exsiccation and seed development. Compared to the N-terminal membrane binding region, the human αsynuclein C-terminus has a greater percentage of charged residues and is polar (Fredenburg et al., 2007). The phosphorylation of this domain occurs on several locations, indicating a regulatory mechanism; nonetheless, the C-terminus function is still unknown, and it is the least conserved domain among α-, β-, and γ- isoforms. Under some circumstances, the C terminus may have an impact on membrane binding; nevertheless, phosphorylation at Ser-87, towards the end of the N-terminal repeats, has a more pronounced effect on membrane binding in vitro than phosphorylation at the other, more C-terminal sites. Thus, the data point to a possible biological function for Ser-87 phosphorylation, however this function in the context of the cell has yet to be determined (Esposito et al., 2007).

2. The Role of Alpha-Synuclein in PD Pathology:

The SNCA gene encipher α-synuclein, a tiny protein that is widely intimate in the central nervous system's presynaptic terminals. Although the precise role of α-synuclein is still largely understood, there is increasing evidence to support the idea that it plays a role in neurotransmitter liberate and synaptic pliability. (Emmanouilidou et al.,2010). Autosomal dominant forms of Parkinson's disease (PD) are commencing by point mutations (A30P, E46K, H50Q, G51D, A53T, and A53E) and duplication or triplication of the SNCA gene; 2) polymorphic variants of the SNCA gene are a significant risk factor for developing idiopathic PD; and 3) Lewy bodies mostly consist of α-synuclein. A drop in the tetramer:monomer ratio and an increase in the number of unfolded monomers of the protein promote the aggregation of α-synuclein. During the aggregation process, α-synuclein changes its shape, adopting a configuration that is rich in beta sheets (Engelender et al., 1999). This shape helps the protein aggregate into oligomers, protofibrils, and insoluble fibrils, which ultimately coalesce into Lewy bodies. The question of whether species of α-synuclein are cytotoxic is hotly debated. While both fibrillar and oligomeric forms of α-synuclein have been demonstrated to be harmful, current research indicates that the more toxic forms that cause cell death in Parkinson's disease are protofibrils and oligomers that develop early in the aggregation process. On the other hand, it seems that α-synuclein fibrils are the most effective in multiplying, which aids in the disease's development and dissemination (Jensen et al., 1999). It is unknown to what degree these oligomers replicate the structure and characteristics of those discovered in brain tissue from Parkinson's disease patients because the majority of investigations that validate the harmful consequences of various a-Syn assemblies have employed in vitro produced species. Mutations, post-translational modifications, a divergence between the α-synuclein synthesis and degradation, and environmental factors all affect a Syn's propensity to aggregate (Jin et al., 2011). The first mutation to be identified was A53T, which is linked to Parkinson's disease with an early start. Predisposing variables for the E46K mutation include a large number of widely distributed Lewy bodies and severe parkinsonism with dementia. These mutations cause the a-Syn protein's structure to alter, which encourages aggregation (Kobayashi et al., 2003). Numerous post-translational changes, including phosphorylation, truncation, ubiquitination, and nitration, occur to α-synuclein. It has been suggested that phosphorylation of α-synuclein induces the formation of cytoplasmic embodiment in some cell culture models, but there is much disagreement over whether phosphorylation plays an active role in α-synuclein aggregation or if it is a response mechanism of cells to try and label and eliminate toxic species of α-synuclein. However, demonstrate that polo-like kinase 2-induced α-Syn phosphorylation controls α-Syn clearance through the lysosomal autophagy route and has no influence on aggregation (Kordower et al., 2008). Phosphorylation and α-synuclein disintegration appear to interact, as evidenced by many lines of accusation. In human neuroblastoma, the inhibition of the ubiquitin-proteasome system or the autophagy-lysosomal pathway led to a significant increase in phosphorylated α-synuclein, suggesting that phosphorylation regulates the degradation of α-Syn (Abeliovich et at., 2000).

3. The Genetics of Parkinson's Disease and Other Disorders Associated With Synucleinopathies:

The mutation reciprocated the amino acid A53T and was associated with a G209A reformation in the SNCA gene that codes for a-synuclein. The illness embodied very early, often in the 40s, and the inheritance pattern was autosomal-dominant. Despite some initial doubt due to the fact that the rodent SNCA homolog's amino acid at position 53 was threonine, this was disregarded when two additional point mutations in SNCA were found, resulting in amino acid changes in A30P and E46K that were linked to autosomal-dominant Parkinson's disease (Al-Chalabi et al., 2009). The next landmark study that linked SNCA to PD through a different mechanism recognized triplications of the SNCA locus in separate families with an autosomal-dominant inheritance pattern (Singleton et al., 2003). As a result, there may have been a total duplication of the a-synuclein burden in these idiopathic, which was subsequently verified at the protein level. Subsequent research manifested duplications of the gene in other families, which were also linked to autosomal-dominant illness (Klucken et al., 2004, Bourdenx et al., 2015). Particular polymorphisms in this region conferred a relative risk for sporadic PD in initial association studies, which were replicated and then confirmed in a large metanalysis (Kordower et al., 2008). Others studies found associations of PD with 30 regions of the gene (Cloug et al., 2009). The confirmation of the relationship between SNCA and sporadic Parkinson's disease (PD) using a large, unbiased GWAS is crucial since targeted association studies are prone to false positives. SNCA has consistently performed well in these investigations, and the 30 area in particular is likely the strongest relationship among those found. From a genetic perspective, rare familial and sporadic PD are both associated with SNCA, according to the findings of these genetic investigations. It is noteworthy that multiple-system atrophy (MSA), another classic synucleinopathy that is always sporadic, has now been linked to SNCA mutations and illness (Desplats et al., 2009).

4. Post Transcriptional Modifications and Interactions of **A**-Synuclein:

Phosphorylation, oxidation, nitrosylation, glycation, or glycosylation are possible modifications for α-synuclein. Phosphorylation is the most well-studied of these changes. Antibodies directed against S129-phosphorylated α-synuclein are a common feature of leukocyte bodies in synucleinopathies. The original theory that this kind of phosphorylation increases α-synuclein inclusions and a-synuclein-soluble oligomers and neurotoxicity is now questioned by other research. Experiments using transgenic flies seem to confirm these conclusions.It is plausible that in LBs that have already formed, S129 phosphorylation—which is minimal under normal circumstances—occurs post-factum (Junn et al., 2009). However, increasing α-synuclein phosphatase activity protected against neurotoxicity induced by a-synuclein, indicating that a-synuclein phosphorylation plays a deleterious causative role in the illness process. The physiological kinases for phosphorylating α-synuclein S129 seem to be Polo-like kinases. Although its clinical relevance is unknown, S87-P a-synuclein, another phosphorylation site for a-synuclein, is also seen inside LBs. Since oxidative/nitrative stress caused by environmental factors, such as mitochondrial toxins, has been strongly linked to Parkinson's disease (PD), α-synuclein oligomerisation induced by oxidation or nitration has garnered interest as a possible point of convergence between environmental and genetic factors that cause the disease. It is important to acknowledge that α-synuclein aggregation may be separated from mitochondrial toxicity-induced death, thereby challenging the idea of oversimplified linear pathways leading to neurodegeneration. Additionally, this raises the question of whether the pathology associated with abundant α-synuclein is sometimes an epiphenomenon rather than a direct cause of neuronal dysfunction and death (Kontopoulus et al., 2006). Similar conclusions may be drawn from research in neurones treated with proteasomal inhibitors, where mortality was not associated with the b-sheetlike pathology of a-synuclein. The α-synuclein carboxy-terminal truncation, which results in fragments lacking some or all of the acidic tail, is another change that may be significant. It seems that fibrillization is more likely to occur in these pieces. One of the enzymes believed to carry out this activity, called calpain, is particularly intriguing because of its localisation in presynaptic terminals and dependency on calcium (Jowaedet al., 2010). Because of its very promiscuous binding characteristics, α-synuclein may bind a variety of proteins in neuronal cells, including dopamine metabolic components like tyrosine hydroxylase (TH) and the dopamine transporter (DAT), so modifying their functions numerous data indicate that α-synuclein may bind to different proteins and therefore have pro- or antiapoptotic effects; nevertheless, no influence on programmed neuronal cell death has been seen in animals lacking α-synuclein. Curiously, though, these mice exhibit resistance to the well-known mitochondrial neurotoxic MPTP via as-yet-unidentified pathways that may entail actions both upstream and downstream from mitochondrial failure. These animals also exhibit resistance to lipopolysaccharide (LPS)-induced nigral degeneration caused by neuro inflammatory, indicating a potential role for endogenous α-synuclein in these death pathways (Klegeris et al., 2008).

5. The Relationship Between A-Synuclein and Oxidative Stress at The Mitochondria:

Numerous investigations have now shown that a fraction of endogenous or overexpressed a-synuclein is present in mitochondria and that it inhibits complex I function. This connects α-synuclein to the consequences of mitochondrial toxins and maybe sporadic Parkinson's disease. Furthermore, α-synuclein transgenic mice have abnormalities in the shape of their brain mitochondria (Hsu et al., 2000). α-Synuclein seems to cause mitochondrial fragmentation, which might lead to later mitochondrial malfunction and death. This fragmentation could take the form of tiny oligomers. Perhaps by the same process of fragmentation, α-synuclein, and especially the mutant version, also causes inappropriate excessive mitophagy, which results in the loss of mitochondria and neuronal death (Hong et al., 2010). A-synuclein has the ability to affect mitochondria, particularly the complex I inhibition, which may lead to the generation of reactive oxygen species (ROS), oxidative stress, and subsequent neuronal death. In fact, there is some evidence that overexpression of a-synuclein can cause reactive oxygen species (ROS), suggesting that pharmacological or molecular methods of blocking these ROS may have neuroprotective benefits in mammalian or insect systems. ER/GOLGI, α-SYNUCLEIN Adenoviral expression of α-synuclein was employed to generate an A53T α-synuclein-mediated neurotoxicity model, wherein Golgi fragmentation was an early characteristic and correlated with the inception of soluble oligomeric species endoplasmic reticulum (ER) stress as an early event. They were also able to inhibit death by exploiting a pharmacological inhibitor of ER stress, indicating that the ER/Golgi may be a primary target of a-synuclein (Esposito et al., 2007). The majority class of modulators of a-synuclein deadly in a blinded screen in a yeast model were found to be genes involved in vesicular trafficking (Doxakis et al., 2010).

6. The Role of Synuclein in Neurotransmitter Release:

Strong evidence for a function in transmitter release has come from the presynaptic position of synuclein and its interactions with membranes. While some of the initial papers said that α-synuclein encourages release, others proposed that it had an inhibitory function. Compared to wild-type animals, α-synuclein knockout mice have a faster recovery from repeated stimulation in dopamine release and a modest reduction in striatal dopamine reserves associated with increased release. The *in vivo* release of norepinephrine and dopamine in mutant mice indicates quicker facilitation and less depression after multiple stimulation bursts compared to wild type. The effects on dopamine release in vivo that have been seen for α-synuclein knockout mice are among the most striking and indicate a significant disruption in the mobilisation of synaptic vesicles. The results at glutamate synapses, however, are considerably less dramatic (Zhang et al.,2005). Non-viral over-expression of the wild type protein often results in little toxicity, despite the fact that over-expression of PD-associated or C-terminal truncation mutations can cause a degenerative process in vivo. Transgenic mice overexpressing the wild type human protein do show several behavioural impairments related to olfaction, gastrointestinal motility, and motor activity, indicating that these animals may recapitulate the prodromal phase of Parkinson's disease, even though there is little to no discernible degeneration (Paleologou et al., 2009). Analysis was expanded to include synaptic physiology and a direct examination of the synuclein gene in order to comprehend how over-expression of synuclein can impact behaviour and result in Parkinson's disease. Direct amperometric recordings of quantal catecholamine release was used to quantify the inhibition of dense core vesicle exocytosis caused by over-expression of the wild type human protein, which was initially investigated in chromaffin cells (Liu et al.,2011). This was a decrease in the quantity of events rather than a change in the kinetics of individual quantal events, quantal size, or calcium sensitivity. In addition, PC12 cell granules seem to gather at the plasma membrane, indicating a particular impairment at or around the fusion event. Considering its impairment in membrane contacts, the A30P mutant's effects were strikingly comparable to those of wild-type human synuclein. By keeping the toxin inside secretory vesicles and away from mitochondria, the vesicular monoamine transporter (VMAT) guards against MPP+ toxicity. The cDNA encoding VMAT was isolated using MPP+ selection. The protection against MPTP toxicity provided by the loss of α-synuclein has been validated by subsequent research, although the extent of this impact appears to vary throughout strains (Cheng et al., 2009). Although MPTP treatment does not alter mitochondria in α-synuclein knockout mice, indicating a deficit in access, monoamine transporters that control toxin admittance appear to officiate similarly in wild type. Thus, resistance to MPTP toxicity is one of the more booming characteristics of the α-synuclein knockout phenotype, while the precise mechanism is yet unknown. The capacity of the α-synuclein deletion to provide protection against the toxin suggests that synuclein's regular function plays a part in the pathophysiology of degeneration, even though MPTP toxicity differs significantly from PD. This is especially true since over-expression of synuclein does not increase vulnerability to MPTP (Lindersson et al.,2004).

7. Misfolding of α-Synuclein:

Aggregates of synuclein have a β-sheet structure, in antithesis to its helical shape on membranes. It is true that α-synuclein makes up the majority, if not all, of the 5–10 nm filaments seen in Lewy bodies and neurites. The acidophilic centre of brainstem-type Lewy bodies labels for α-synuclein less strongly than the pale-staining halo, which by electron microscopy comprises filaments. Filaments comparable to those found in less distinct Lewy bodies of the cortical type are found in dystrophic neuritis (Winslow et al., 2010). Even though the fact that Lewy bodies were once thought to be a byproduct of the degenerative process, the discovery of α-synuclein mutations in familial Parkinson's disease (PD) indicated that the main cause of Lewy-related pathology was genetic. It's crucial to keep in mind, though, that this is not the same as proving that Lewy pathology is a cause of the degenerative process. Following a lengthy in vitro incubation time, filaments are also formed by recombinant synuclein. These filaments take on the typical amyloid cross-beta structure by X-ray diffraction. In addition, high-resolution analysis of fibrils using recent solid-state NMR has started to reveal the repeating units underlying this structure (Xilomi et al., 2008). Since aggregation is believed to be the keystone event in the aetiology of Parkinson's disease, the in vitro test has received a lot of attention. The point mutations A53T, A30P, and E46K associated with familial Parkinson disease (PD) were formerly assumed to accelerate aggregation; however, while oligomerisation may be enhanced, the A30P mutant seems to produce fibrils more slowly than the wild type. As previously mentioned, β- and γ-synuclein have the ability to stop α-synuclein from aggregating both in vitro and in vivo; yet, they may also cause disease, suggesting that the tendency to aggregate does not always equate to the capacity to cause degeneration. Fibrillization is absent in β-synuclein (Ostrerova et al., 1999).

8. Conclusions:

It was discovered more than twenty years ago that the primary composing of Lewy bodies is α-Syn. Since then, this protein has gained recognition as a potential treatment target and PD diagnostic biomarker. Additionally, this protein has been employed in several animal models to try and replicate Parkinson's disease. While many parts to the pathology of Parkinson's disease (PD) in humans may be replicated in animal models, none of them can replicate all of the illness's distinctive pathological and clinical hallmarks. The difficulty of recreating Parkinson's disease (PD) in animal models is reflected in the lack of similar phenotypes between mice interjaculate with lethal a-Syn species and rodents overexpressing a-Syn. It seems adequate to just raise the quantity of αsynuclein, although its interaction with membranes is likely to be important. Reduced synuclein levels support its physiological function at the nerve terminal by either directly (as a chaperone) or indirectly (via other effects on the synaptic vesicle cycle) reducing the quantity of SNARE complex. Synuclein may goal other membranes, such as the mitochondria, when it is up-regulated through physiological or pathological pathways. This likely explains the toxicity seen in Parkinson's disease (PD) in humans. Thus, it would seem that synuclein's interaction with membranes is essential to both its normal function and its role in decadence. Understanding how this synergy affects synuclein's shape will aid in our understanding of the misfolding that takes place in Parkinson's disease. All of these issues, though, will need to be answered by more effective ways to comprehend how synuclein functions inside cells.

Conflict of interest: The authors declare that there is no conflict of interest

References:

1. Abeliovich, A., Schmitz, Y., Farinas, I., Choi-Lundberg, D., Ho, W. H., Castillo, P. E., Shinsky, N., Verdugo, J. M., Armanini, M., Ryan, A., et al. (2000). Mice lacking α-synuclein display functional deficits in the nigrostriatal dopamine system. Neuron, 25, 239–252.

2. Albert, K., Voutilainen, M. H., Domanskyi, A., & Airavaara, M. (2017). AAV vector-mediated gene delivery to substantia nigra dopamine neurons: Implications for gene therapy and disease models. Genes, 8(2), 63. https://doi.org/10.3390/genes8020063

3. Al-Chalabi, A., Dürr, A., Wood, N. W., Parkinson, M. H., Camuzat, A., Hulot, J. S., Morrison, K. E., Renton, A., Sussmuth, S. D., Landwehrmeyer, B. G., et al. (2009). Genetic variants of the α-synuclein gene SNCA are associated with multiple system atrophy. PLoS One, 4, e7114.

4. Alim, M. A., Hossain, M. S., Arima, K., Takeda, K., Izumiyama, Y., Nakamura, M., Kaji, H., Shinoda, T., Hisanaga, S., & Ueda, K. (2002). Tubulin seeds α-synuclein fibril formation. Journal of Biological Chemistry, 277, 2112–2117.

5. Alim, M. A., Ma, Q. L., Takeda, K., Aizawa, T., Matsubara, M., Nakamura, M., Asada, A., Saito, T., Kaji, H., Yoshii, M., et al. (2004). Demonstration of a role for α-synuclein as a functional microtubule-associated protein. Journal of Alzheimer's Disease, 6, 435–442.

6.   Alvarez-Erviti, L., Rodriguez-Oroz, M. C., Cooper, J. M., Caballero, C., Ferrer, I., Obeso, J. A., & Schapira, A. H. (2010). Chaperone-mediated autophagy markers in Parkinson disease brains. Archives of Neurology, 67, 1464–1472.

7.   Al-Wandi, A., Ninkina, N., Millership, S., Williamson, S. J., Jones, P. A., & Buchman, V. L. (2010). Absence of α-synuclein affects dopamine metabolism and synaptic markers in the striatum of aging mice. Neurobiology of Aging, 31, 796–804.

8.   Bengoa-Vergniory, N., Roberts, R. F., Wade-Martins, R., & Alegre-Abarrategui, J. (2017). Alpha-synuclein oligomers: A new hope. Acta Neuropathologica, 134(6), 819–838. https://doi.org/10.1007/s00401-017-1755-1

9.   Bolam, J. P., & Pissadaki, E. K. (2012). Living on the edge with too many mouths to feed: Why dopamine neurons die. Movement Disorders, 27(12), 1478–1483. https://doi.org/10.1002/mds.25135

10. Bourdenx, M., Dovero, S., Engeln, M., Bido, S., Bastide, M. F., Dutheil, N., et al. (2015). Lack of additive role of ageing in nigrostriatal neurodegeneration triggered by α-synuclein overexpression. Acta Neuropathologica Communications, 3, 46. https://doi.org/10.1186/s40478-015-0222-2

11. Braak, H., Del Tredici, K., Rüb, U., De Vos, R. A. I., Jansen Steur, E. N. H., & Braak, E. (2003). Staging of brain pathology related to sporadic Parkinson's disease. Neurobiology of Aging, 24(2), 197–211. https://doi.org/10.1016/S0197-4580(02)00065-9

12. Chu, Y., & Kordower, J. H. (2007). Age-associated increases of α-synuclein in monkeys and humans are associated with nigrostriatal dopamine depletion: Is this the target for Parkinson's disease? Neurobiology of Disease, 25, 134–149.

13. Chung, C. Y., Koprich, J. B., Siddiqi, H., & Isacson, O. (2009). Dynamic changes in presynaptic and axonal transport proteins combined with striatal neuroinflammation precede dopaminergic neuronal loss in a rat model of AAV α-synucleinopathy. Journal of Neuroscience, 29, 3365–3373.

14. Clark, J., Clore, E. L., Zheng, K., Adame, A., Masliah, E., & Simon, D. K. (2010). Oral N-acetyl-cysteine attenuates loss of dopaminergic terminals in α-synuclein overexpressing mice. PLoS One, 5, e12333.

15. Clough, R. L., Dermentzaki, G., & Stefanis, L. (2009). Functional dissection of the α-synuclein promoter: Transcriptional regulation by ZSCAN21 and ZNF219. Journal of Neurochemistry, 110, 1479–1490.

16. Darios, F., Ruipérez, V., López, I., Villanueva, J., Gutierrez, L. M., & Davletov, B. (2010). α-Synuclein sequesters arachidonic acid to modulate SNARE-mediated exocytosis. EMBO Reports, 11(7), 528–533.

17. Dauer, W., Kholodilov, N., Vila, M., Trillat, A. C., Goodchild, R., Larsen, K. E., Staal, R., Tieu, K., Schmitz, Y., & Yuan, C. A., et al. (2002). Resistance of α-synuclein null mice to the parkinsonian neurotoxin MPTP. Proceedings of the National Academy of Sciences, 99, 14524–14529.

18. Desplats, P., Lee, H. J., Bae, E. J., Patrick, C., Rockenstein, E., Crews, L., Spencer, B., Masliah, E., & Lee, S. J. (2009). Inclusion formation and neuronal cell death through neuron-to-neuron transmission of α-synuclein. Proceedings of the National Academy of Sciences, 106, 13010–13015.

19. Desplats, P., Spencer, B., Coffee, E., Patel, P., Michael, S., Patrick, C., Adame, A., Rockenstein, E., & Masliah, E. (2011). α-Synuclein sequesters Dnmt1 from the nucleus: A novel mechanism for epigenetic alterations in Lewy body diseases. Journal of Biological Chemistry, 286, 9031–9037.

20. Doxakis, E. (2010). Post-transcriptional regulation of α-synuclein expression by mir-7 and mir-153. Journal of Biological Chemistry, 285(17), 12726–12734.

21. Eliezer, P., Zweckstetter, D., Masliah, M., & Lashuel, E. H. A. (2010). Phosphorylation at S87 is enhanced in synucleinopathies, inhibits α-synuclein oligomerization, and influences synuclein-membrane interactions. Journal of Neuroscience, 30, 3184–3198.

22. Emmanouilidiou, E., Elenis, D., Papasilekas, T., Stranjalis, G., Gerozissis, K., Ioannou, P., & Vekrellis, K. (2011). In vivo assessment of α-synuclein secretion. PLoS One, 6, e22225.

23. Emmanouilidou, E., Melachroinou, K., Roumeliotis, T., Garbis, S. D., Ntzouni, M., Margaritis, L. H., Stefanis, L., & Vekrellis, K. (2010b). Cell-produced α-synuclein is secreted in a calcium-dependent manner by exosomes and impacts neuronal survival. Journal of Neuroscience, 30, 6838–6851.

24. Emmanouilidou, E., Stefanis, L., & Vekrellis, K. (2010a). Specific cell-derived soluble α-synuclein oligomers are degraded by the 26S proteasome and impair its function. Neurobiology of Aging, 31, 953–968.

25. Engelender, S., Kaminsky, Z., Guo, X., Sharp, A. H., Amaravi, R. K., Kleiderlein, J. J., Margolis, R. L., Troncoso, J. C., Lanahan, A. A., & Worley, P. F., et al. (1999). Synphilin-1 associates with α-synuclein and promotes the formation of cytosolic inclusions. Nature Genetics, 22, 110–114.

26. Esposito, A., Dohm, C. P., Kermer, P., Bahr, M., & Wouters, F. S. (2007). α-Synuclein and its disease-related mutants interact differentially with the microtubule protein tau and associate with the actin cytoskeleton. Neurobiology of Disease, 26, 521–531.

27. Fredenburg, R. A., Rospigliosi, C., Meray, R. K., Kessler, J. C., Lashuel, H. A., Eliezer, D., & Lansbury, P. T., Jr. (2007). The impact of the E46K mutation on the properties of α-synuclein in its monomeric and oligomeric states. Biochemistry, 46, 7107–7118.

28. Fuchs, J., Nilsson, C., Kachergus, J., Munz, M., Larsson, E. M., Schule, B., Langston, J. W., Middleton, F. A., Ross, O. A., & Hulihan, M., et al. (2007). Phenotypic variation in a large Swedish pedigree due to SNCA duplication and triplication. Neurology, 68, 916–922.

29. Hong, Z., Shi, M., Chung, K. A., Quinn, J. F., Peskind, E. R., Galasko, D., Jankovic, J., Zabetian, C. P., Leverenz, J. B., Baird, G., et al. (2010). DJ-1 and α-synuclein in human cerebrospinal fluid as biomarkers of Parkinson's disease. Brain, 133(3), 713–726.

30. Hsu, L. J., Sagara, Y., Arroyo, A., Rockenstein, E., Sisk, A., Mallory, M., Wong, J., Takenouchi, T., Hashimoto, M., & Masliah, E. (2000). α-Synuclein promotes mitochondrial deficit and oxidative stress. American Journal of Pathology, 157, 401–410.

31. Inglis, K. J., Chereau, D., Brigham, E. F., Chiou, S. S., Schöbel, S., Frigon, N. L., Yu, M., Caccavello, R. J., Nelson, S., & Motter, R., et al. (2009). Polo-like kinase 2 (PLK2) phosphorylates α-synuclein at serine 129 in central nervous system. Journal of Biological Chemistry, 284, 2598–2602.

32. Dickson, D. W., Uchikado, H., Fujishiro, H., & Tsuboi, Y. (2010). Evidence in favor of Braak staging of Parkinson's disease. Movement Disorders, 25(Suppl 1), S78–S82.

33. Jowaed, A., Schmitt, I., Kaut, O., & Wüllner, U. (2010). Methylation regulates α-synuclein expression and is decreased in Parkinson's disease patients' brains. Journal of Neuroscience, 30, 6355–6359.

34. Jensen, P. H., Hager, H., Nielsen, M. S., Hojrup, P., Gliemann, J., & Jakes, R. (1999). α-Synuclein binds to τ and stimulates the protein kinase A-catalyzed phosphorylation of serine residues 262 and 356. Journal of Biological Chemistry, 274, 25481–25489.

35. Junn, E., Lee, K. W., Jeong, B. S., Chan, T. W., Im, J. Y., & Mouradian, M. M. (2009). Repression of α-synuclein expression and toxicity by microRNA-7. Proceedings of the National Academy of Sciences, 106, 13052–13057.

36. Klegeris, A., Pelech, S., Giasson, B. I., Maguire, J., Zhang, H., McGeer, E. G., & McGeer, P. L. (2008). α-Synuclein activates stress signaling protein kinases in THP-1 cells and microglia. Neurobiology of Aging, 29, 739–752.

37. Klucken, J., Shin, Y., Masliah, E., Hyman, B. T., & McLean, P. J. (2004). Hsp70 reduces α-synuclein aggregation and toxicity. Journal of Biological Chemistry, 279, 25497–25502.

38. Kobayashi, H., Krüger, R., Markopoulou, K., Wszolek, Z., Chase, B., Taka, H., Mineki, R., Murayama, K., Riess, O., & Mizuno, Y., et al. (2003). Haploinsufficiency at the α-synuclein gene underlies phenotypic severity in familial Parkinson's disease. Brain, 126(Pt 1), 32–42.

39. Kontopoulos, E., Parvin, J. D., & Feany, M. B. (2006). α-Synuclein acts in the nucleus to inhibit histone acetylation and promote neurotoxicity. Human Molecular Genetics, 15, 3012–3023.

40. Kordower, J. H., Chu, Y., Hauser, R. A., Freeman, T. B., & Olanow, C. W. (2008). Lewy body-like pathology in long-term embryonic nigral transplants in Parkinson's disease. Nature Medicine, 14, 504–506.

41. Kostka, M., Högen, T., Danzer, K. M., Levin, J., Habeck, M., Wirth, A., Wagner, R., Glabe, C. G., Finger, S., & Heinzelmann, U., et al. (2008). Single particle characterization of iron-induced pore-forming α-synuclein oligomers. Journal of Biological Chemistry, 283, 10992–11003.

42. Kotzbauer, P. T., Giasson, B. I., Kravitz, A. V., Golbe, L. I., Mark, M. H., Trojanowski, J. Q., & Lee, V. M. (2004). Fibrillization of α-synuclein and tau in familial Parkinson's disease caused by the A53T α-synuclein mutation. Experimental Neurology, 187, 279–288.

43. Lindersson, E., Beedholm, R., Højrup, P., Moos, T., Gai, W., Hendil, K. B., & Jensen, P. H. (2004). Proteasomal inhibition by α-synuclein filaments and oligomers. Journal of Biological Chemistry, 279, 12924–12934.

44. Linnertz, C., Saucier, L., Ge, D., Cronin, K. D., Burke, J. R., Browndyke, J. N., Hulette, C. M., Welsh-Bohmer, K. A., & Chiba-Falek, O. (2009). Genetic regulation of α-synuclein mRNA expression in various human brain tissues. PLoS One, 4, e7480.

45. Liu, F., Nguyen, J. L., Hulleman, J. D., Li, L., & Rochet, J. C. (2008). Mechanisms of DJ-1 neuroprotection in a cellular model of Parkinson's disease. Journal of Neurochemistry, 105, 2435–2453.

46. Liu, G., Zhang, C., Yin, J., Li, X., Cheng, F., Li, Y., Yang, H., Ueda, K., Chan, P., & Yu, S. (2009). α-Synuclein is differentially expressed in mitochondria from different rat brain regions and dose-dependently down-regulates complex I activity. Neuroscience Letters, 454, 187–192.

47. Liu, Z., Yu, Y., Li, X., Ross, C. A., & Smith, W. W. (2011). Curcumin protects against A53T α-synuclein-induced toxicity in a PC12 inducible cell model for Parkinsonism. Pharmacological Research, 63, 439–444.

48. Ostrerova, N., Petrucelli, L., Farrer, M., Mehta, N., Choi, P., Hardy, J., & Wolozin, B. (1999). α-Synuclein shares physical and functional homology with 14–3–3 proteins. Journal of Neuroscience, 19, 5782–5791.

49. Ostrerova-Golts, N., Petrucelli, L., Hardy, J., Lee, J. M., Farer, M., & Wolozin, B. (2000). The A53T α-synuclein mutation increases iron-dependent aggregation and toxicity. Journal of Neuroscience, 20, 6048–6054.

50. Paleologou, K. E., Kragh, C. L., Mann, D. M., Salem, S. A., Al-Shami, R., Allsop, D., Hassan, A. H., Jensen, P. H., & El-Agnaf, O. M. (2009). Detection of elevated levels of soluble α-synuclein oligomers in post-mortem brain extracts from patients with dementia with Lewy bodies. Brain, 132(Pt 4), 1093–1101.

51. Winslow, A. R., Chen, C. W., Corrochano, S., Acevedo-Arozena, A., Gordon, D. E., Peden, A. A., Lichtenberg, M., Menzies, F. M., Ravikumar, B., & Imarisio, S., et al. (2010). α-Synuclein impairs macroautophagy: Implications for Parkinson's disease. Journal of Cell Biology, 190, 1023–1037.

52. Withers, G. S., George, J. M., Banker, G. A., & Clayton, D. F. (1997). Delayed localization of synelfin (synuclein, NACP) to presynaptic terminals in cultured rat hippocampal neurons. Brain Research Developmental Brain Research, 99, 87–94.

53. Xilouri, M., Vogiatzi, T., Vekrellis, K., & Stefanis, L. (2008). α-Synuclein degradation by autophagic pathways: A potential key to Parkinson's disease pathogenesis. Autophagy, 4, 917–919.

54. Zhang, W., Wang, T., Pei, Z., Miller, D. S., Wu, X., Block, M. L., Wilson, B., Zhang, W., Zhou, Y., & Hong, J. S., et al. (2005). Aggregated α-synuclein activates microglia: A process leading to disease progression in Parkinson's disease. FASEB Journal, 19, 533–542.

3. GEOSPATIAL ASSESSMENT OF URBANIZATION TRENDS IN INDIA: PATTERNS, CHALLENGES, AND FUTURE PERSPECTIVES

Pranoy Dey

Assistant Professor, Department of Geography, Birpara College

Alipurduar, West Bengal, Pin- 735204

Email: pranoy.dey93@gmail.com

Abstract:

Urbanization is a transforming phenomenon having substantial consequences for social, economic, and environmental systems. This report offers a thorough geographical examination of urbanization developments in India, emphasizing the patterns, difficulties, and future prospects. The author analyzes the spatial distribution and expansion of urban areas throughout various parts of the country using remote sensing data, Geographic Information Systems (GIS) techniques, and statistical analysis. This article delineates certain urbanization tendencies marked by swift growth in particular metropolitan regions, alongside varying rates of peri-urban development. The author identifies the principal factors of urbanization, including population growth, rural-urban movement, and economic activities. Nonetheless, the report underscores other issues stemming from unregulated urbanization, including insufficient infrastructure, housing deficits, environmental deterioration, and socioeconomic disparities. The author seeks to clarify the geographical aspects of urbanization trends, difficulties, and future prospects to facilitate informed policies that encourage harmonious urban development in the quickly changing Indian context.

Keywords: Geographical analysis, Urbanization, Urban development

1. Introduction

Urbanization, characterized by the growth of urban populations and the expansion of metropolitan territories, is a pivotal phenomenon of the contemporary era, influencing cultures, economies, and landscapes globally. In the Indian context, urbanization has assumed a multifaceted nature, propelled by a complex interaction of demographic, economic, and social factors. As one of the most populous and culturally diverse nations, India's urbanization patterns have distinct significance, providing a complex array of difficulties, possibilities, and promises. In recent decades, India has experienced a significant transition as rural inhabitants relocate to urban areas in pursuit of enhanced livelihoods and a superior quality of life. This phenomenon has resulted in the swift proliferation of metropolitan regions, frequently exceeding the ability of cities to deliver fundamental services and infrastructure. As urban areas expand, they present numerous issues, including housing shortages, transportation congestion, environmental deterioration, and socioeconomic inequalities. This study conducts a thorough geographical analysis of urbanization patterns in India, seeking to elucidate the spatial dynamics, trends, difficulties, and future prospects inherent to this revolutionary process. Utilizing new geospatial technologies, including remote sensing and Geographic Information Systems (GIS), the author investigates the complex interconnections between urban expansion, land use alterations, and socioeconomic variables throughout various parts of the nation.

This research has three objectives: first, to map and analyze the spatial distribution of urban areas, identifying urbanization hotspots and their expansion trajectories; second, to investigate the underlying drivers of urbanization, including population growth, rural-urban migration's, economic activities, and infrastructure development; and third, to critically evaluate the challenges associated with rapid urbanization, such as infrastructure deficits, environmental impacts, and social inequalities. This study aims to delineate the trajectory of India's urban future. The author aims to offer insights into the sustainable and inclusive evolution of India's cities by projecting alternative scenarios and imagining the impact of new urban planning strategies, technological interventions, and governmental efforts. As urbanization increasingly influences the nation's terrain, comprehending its geographical aspects is essential for informed decision-making and the attainment of comprehensive, equitable urban development. The author will examine the methodological framework for spatial analysis, present empirical findings from the analyses, and discuss the implications for policy formulation, urban planning, and future research directions in the following sections of this research. Through this thorough analysis, the author seeks to enhance the current dialogue on Indian urbanization and offer a nuanced comprehension of its complex character.

The geographical analysis examines the future prospects of urbanization in India, taking into account probable scenarios and policy ramifications. The author examines the significance of sustainable urban design, smart city initiatives, and technological integration in tackling urban difficulties and promoting equitable development. The study highlights the significance of spatially-informed decision-making in controlling urbanization and promoting resilient, inclusive, and ecologically sustainable cities. This study enhances the comprehension of India's urbanization dynamics, providing significant insights for policymakers, urban planners, and researchers.

2. Literature Review:

The literature on the geographical analysis of urbanization patterns in India offers a thorough understanding of the intricacies and dynamics involved in this transforming process. Scholars have provided vital insights for sustainable urban development through empirical investigations, theoretical frameworks, and policy recommendations. As India's urbanization progresses, interdisciplinary research and spatial analysis will be crucial for understanding the changing urban environment and facilitating informed decision-making. Prior investigations into the geographical examination of urbanization patterns in India have yielded significant insights into trends, difficulties, and future prospects of urban growth. Presented below are significant studies and research findings in this domain:

"India's Urban Awakening: Constructing Inclusive Cities, Sustaining Economic Growth" (World Bank, 2019): This detailed paper analyzes urbanization trends in India and underscores the need of inclusive urban development. The text addresses the issues posed by growing urbanization, such as infrastructure deficiencies and socioeconomic disparities, and offers policy proposals for sustainable urban development. The research "Urbanization in India: Trends, Opportunities, and Challenges" (UNDP, 2019) examines the economic and social aspects of urbanization in India, emphasizing the difficulties of managing urban expansion while promoting social fairness and environmental sustainability. It underscores the necessity for cohesive urban planning and investment in infrastructure. "Urbanisation and Health in India" (The Lancet, 2017): This research paper examines the health consequences of urbanization in India. The text examines the effects of urban living on health outcomes, encompassing access to healthcare services, environmental pollution, and communicable diseases. The research emphasizes the significance of incorporating health issues into urban design.

The paper "Urbanization and Governance in India" (International Journal of Urban and Regional Research, 2016) analyzes the governance problems linked to urbanization in India. It examines the function of local governments, urban policies, and institutional frameworks in regulating urban expansion and fulfilling the requirements of urban inhabitants. This study examines the environmental impacts of urbanization in India. This study examines the correlation between urbanization and air and water pollution, emphasizing the necessity for sustainable urban development policies to alleviate environmental consequences.

"Urbanization, Industrialization, and the Environment: A Comparative Analysis of India and China" (World Development, 2014): This paper examines the urbanization and industrialization processes in India and China and their environmental repercussions. It examines policy strategies to reconcile economic development with environmental conservation. This study examines the spatial patterns of urbanization in India and finds the factors influencing urban expansion. It examines elements including economic development, population dynamics, and infrastructural investments that affect urbanization trends.

3. Urbanization Patterns in India:

Urbanization has been extensively researched, particularly in fast developing nations such as India. The body of literature on Indian urbanization encompasses multiple disciplines, including geography, urban planning, economics, sociology, and environmental science. This literature review seeks to furnish an analysis of principal themes, conclusions, and discussions regarding the geographical examination of urbanization patterns in India, emphasizing trends, difficulties, and future opportunities.

3.1. Urbanization Trends and Patterns: Research has recorded the spatial distribution of urban regions throughout India, uncovering diverse patterns of urban expansion. Urban agglomerations, especially as metropolitan regions, have undergone considerable expansion due to rural-to-urban migration and natural population increase. The aforementioned tendencies have resulted in the development of peri-urban zones marked by intricate land use dynamics and hybrid rural-urban landscapes.

3.2. Factors Influencing Urbanization: The research highlights various factors driving urbanization in India. Accelerated population growth, together with rural-to-urban migration motivated by economic ambitions and job prospects, has been a principal driver of urban expansion. Furthermore, the transition of economic activities from agriculture to manufacturing and services has facilitated the transformation of rural areas into urban centers.

3.3. Challenges of Rapid Urbanization: Urbanization in India has presented numerous challenges. Insufficient infrastructure, encompassing housing, sanitation, and transportation, continues to be a significant issue in numerous urban areas. Environmental degradation, air and water pollution, and the depletion of green spaces are direct outcomes of unregulated urban expansion. The proliferation of informal settlements intensifies socioeconomic disparities, resulting in poverty, unequal service access, and social exclusion.

3.4. Environmental Impacts: The research underscores the ecological repercussions of urbanization, especially for India's distinctive ecosystems. Research has investigated the effects of urban sprawl on regional ecosystems, water supplies, and biodiversity. The expansion of urban areas into ecologically sensitive regions, including coastal zones and forested landscapes, has generated apprehensions over sustainable land use and conservation.

3.5. Policy Interventions and Future Outlook: Academics and policymakers have investigated diverse solutions to tackle the issues presented by urbanization. Initiatives for sustainable urban design, the advancement of smart cities, and the incorporation of technology for effective resource management have garnered significant attention. The literature underscores the necessity for inclusive urban development, prioritizing affordable housing, enhanced public services, and social fairness.

3.6. Geospatial Analysis and Remote Sensing: Geospatial technologies, such as remote sensing and Geographic Information Systems (GIS), have been important in comprehending urbanization patterns and dynamics. Remote sensing data have been utilized to monitor land use alterations, delineate urban expansion, and evaluate the effects of urbanization on the environment. GIS-based spatial analysis elucidates the spatial linkages between metropolitan regions and diverse socio-economic variables.

3.7. Knowledge Gaps and Future Research: Despite considerable progress, there remain knowledge gaps that necessitate additional inquiry. Longitudinal studies monitoring urbanization patterns over time, comprehensive evaluations of particular urban concerns, and interdisciplinary methodologies that integrate social, economic, and environmental aspects necessitate further investigation.

4. Trends, Challenges and Future Prospects:

4.1. Current Trends:

- **Rapid Urbanization:** India has been undergoing substantial urbanization, characterized by a marked migration of inhabitants from rural areas to urban centers. This has resulted in the proliferation of urban agglomerations and the formation of novel urban centers.
- **Megacities and Metropolises:** Prominent cities such as Mumbai, Delhi, and Bengaluru have experienced rapid population expansion, leading to the emergence of megacities

and metropolises. These metropolitan areas function as economic magnets yet encounter issues with infrastructure and resource management.

- **Peri-Urban Growth**: In conjunction with metropolitan centers, peri-urban regions — the transitional areas between urban and rural – have experienced significant growth. These regions frequently encounter a combination of land uses and have distinct issues regarding planning and development.

- **Technology and Smart Cities**: The integration of technology and the notion of smart cities has accelerated. Cities are utilizing digital technologies for urban planning, transit management, and public service provision.

4.2. Challenges:

- **Infrastructure Deficiencies**: Accelerated urbanization has burdened current infrastructure, resulting in insufficient housing, inadequate sanitation facilities, and traffic congestion. Numerous urban regions are deficient in fundamental services, thus affecting people' quality of life.

- **Environmental Degradation**: Urban expansion has resulted in environmental issues including air and water pollution, deforestation, and the reduction of green spaces. These concerns affect public health and the comprehensive sustainability of urban areas.

- **Social Inequalities**: Urbanization has intensified social disparities, with informal settlements frequently devoid of essential services, education, and healthcare. This urban disparity may incite social discontent and impede equitable development.

- **Water and Resource Scarcity**: The expansion of urban populations amplifies the demand for water and other resources. Water scarcity, along with ineffective resource management, is a considerable obstacle to sustaining urban development.

4.3. Prospective Outlook:

- **Sustainable Urban Planning**: Future urban development necessitates a robust emphasis on sustainable planning, integrating principles of compact urban design, mixed land use, and efficient resource management.

- **Inclusive Cities**: Initiatives aimed at fostering inclusivity in urban environments will progressively intensify. Cities are expected to invest in green infrastructure projects, such as urban parks, green belts, and sustainable transportation systems, to reduce environmental consequences and improve citizens' well-being.

- **Climate Resilience:** In light of the problems presented by climate change, urban areas must bolster their resilience through the adoption of climate-adaptive methods, including flood management systems and sustainable drainage solutions.
- **Digital Transformation:** The incorporation of technology will persist in influencing urban environments, characterized by the proliferation of smart city initiatives, digital governance, and data-informed decision-making.
- **Decentralization and Regional Development:** To mitigate the strain on megacities, there may be a heightened focus on fostering regional development and decentralization, boosting growth in smaller metropolitan centers.

In summary, the trends, problems, and future prospects of the geographical analysis of urbanization patterns in India illustrate a complex interaction among rapid urban expansion, environmental issues, social dynamics, and technological progress. Confronting difficulties while leveraging possibilities necessitates diverse strategies, evidence-based policies, and a dedication to developing sustainable, inclusive, and resilient urban environments.Crucial, tackling social disparities with policies that ensure affordable housing, equitable service access, and economic opportunities for everyone.

5. Conclusion:

In conclusion, the regional examination of urbanization trends in India provides a deep insight into the complex shift the country is experiencing. This study elucidates the trends, difficulties, and future prospects that underscore the urgency and complexity of managing urban expansion in a swiftly evolving environment. As the process of urbanization intensifies, it is clear that deliberate and purposeful measures are essential to develop cities that are sustainable, inclusive, and attuned to the requirements of their residents. This analysis highlights the rapid rate of urban growth, resulting in the formation of megacities and the transformation of peri-urban regions. These patterns are influenced by a convergence of factors, including demographic changes, rural-urban migration, and economic prospects. Nevertheless, in conjunction with these advances, difficulties have emerged, threatening the fundamental structure of urban growth. The issues of insufficient infrastructure, environmental deterioration, socioeconomic disparities, and resource constraint require urgent intervention. Confronting these difficulties necessitates a fundamental transformation in urban planning and governance. Sustainable urban development must serve as the foundation of policy initiatives, guaranteeing that cities are constructed for efficiency, resilience, and inclusivity. Moreover, recognizing the significance of social fairness and environmental stewardship is essential for developing communities that improve the quality of life for all residents. The future outlook for Indian urbanization is both optimistic and challenging. Sustainable urban planning will be crucial in determining the course of urban development. The incorporation of technology, the advancement of green infrastructure, and the enhancement of climate resilience will be essential in realizing this objective. Furthermore, a decentralized strategy for urban development, prioritizing regional expansion and equitable distribution, might mitigate the strain on large metropolitan centers and provide more equitable possibilities across. In the comprehensive narrative of India's urbanization, each element signifies a distinct difficulty or opportunity. By integrating sustainable development, social fairness, and environmental awareness, India can create cities that exemplify growth and harmony. This necessitates cooperative efforts by politicians, urban planners, researchers, and citizens – a unified initiative to guide India's urbanization towards a future where cities flourish as vibrant hubs of innovation, culture, and human welfare. The geographical examination of urbanization patterns in India provides insight, directing the way towards a more resilient and affluent urban future.

References:

1. Angel, S., & Parent, J. (2011). *Cities and urbanization: Understanding the geography of India's urban transformation.* International Growth Centre.
2. Bhagat, R. B., & Singh, A. (2012). Urbanization and urban systems in India. *Economic and Political Weekly, 47*(14), 43-52.
3. Chandramouli, C. (2011). *Census of India 2011: Provisional population totals, paper 1 of 2011: India series 1.* Office of the Registrar General & Census Commissioner, India.
4. Dhar, A. (2015). Urbanization and environmental quality in India. *Ecological Economics, 120,* 125-137.
5. Government of India. (2015). *National Urban Information System.* Ministry of Urban Development.
6. Mahadevia, D., & Raju, S. (Eds.). (2019). *India's urban transformation: 2011-2019.* Oxford University Press.
7. Ramachandra, T. V., & Bharath, H. A. (2015). Spatio-temporal characteristics of urbanisation in India. *Journal of Environmental Science, Computer Science and Engineering & Technology, 4*(4), 341-358.
8. Satterthwaite, D. (2007). *The transition to a predominantly urban world and its underpinnings.* Human Settlements Discussion Paper Series: Urban Change, 3.

4. DIGITAL LIVES: HOW SOCIAL MEDIA SHAPES YOUTH MENTAL WELLBEING

***Nikhil Zebukumar, ** Prof. (Dr.) C Jayan**

*Research Scholar, Department of Psychology, University of Kerala, Thiruvananthapuram, Kerala.

** Visiting Professor, Department of Psychology, University of Kerala, Thiruvananthapuram, Kerala

Email id: nikhilzebu1998@gmail.com

Abstract:

The present study investigated the Social Media Usage and Mental Wellbeing among Young Adults. The data was collected from 154 young adults consisting from different districts of Kerala, using Warwick Edinburgh Mental Well-being Scale and **The Bergen Social Media Addiction Scale**. The findings of the study revealed that Social Media Usage has a negative correlation with Mental Wellbeing. The study provides insights about how social media usage relates to mental wellbeing. This study may be treated as a starting point in helping researchers understand and identify the social media usage and mental wellbeing among Young Adults. Findings of the study can be used for understanding the dynamic of the study variables and helps to develop more effective strategies to manage the social media overuse among youth. Further studies incorporating developing intervention will be helpful in overcoming the difficulties of social media addiction.

Keywords: Social Media Usage, Mental Wellbeing, Young Adults

1. Introduction:

India has 5.52 billion active Internet users as of 2024 and approximately 462 million active social media accounts showing the growth of social media users (Petrosyan, 2024). Social media has captured millions of users worldwide within a small span of years. Social media has been referred to as "social media sites" or a set of information technologies which facilitate interactions and networking (Diga and Kelleher, 2009). Social media is a ubiquitous medium in present scenario due to its capability over instant information transfer and communication with people using the internet connection. The prospects of communication have immensely widened because of social media. They have an apparent impact on our social, political, economic and ideological realms.

It does touch every sphere of life like, economy, policy formulation, politics, marketing, personal and social life. Social media equips in learning, awareness, education and information. The advancement of smartphones marked   revolution in instant communication and data sharing. There are many social media platforms like Facebook, TikTok , Pinterest, WhatsApp, Snapchat, Telegram, Twitter and Instagram that make it easier for people spread across the globe to connect. Social media act as a great device for education, as they can access live lectures and post, share and avail feedback from the institutions and as well as from tutors. Social media posits a change in seeking news, people can get updated over the latest happenings of world through social media. Social media is a platform for digital marketing and e-commerce, it benefits advertisement industry for branding and promotion.

2. Impact of Social Media on Youth:

However social media usage has a pivotal role in our generation it has apparent negative side too. Social media usage refers to online behaviours that facilitate "direct exchanges" among users. Such behaviours include liking, commenting, sending messages, and otherwise engaging with other users (Kaplan and Haenlein, 2010). Younger adults and teenagers are most affected with addiction as they waste their personal valuable time that can be vested in productive activities. Addiction points to extensive involvement and eventually cut off from the environment. Social media became a repository for fake news and propaganda, many eminent persons lost their reputation over the fake news that spread across timelines. There are many cybercrimes in the country which include personal revenge, fraud, sexual exploitation, inciting hate, piracy, stealing information, etc. In some cases, social media handles glamourize alcohol and drug use. Misleading messages pretending as health advices attune to unaware social media users.

Cyberbullying is another devastating menace that amalgamates with social media. At present greater number of females and children are victimized through cyber stalking and bullying. Bullying over social media is open to public and it does have permanent effects on victims. Anything said and done online can never be erased entirely, causing potentially permanent damage to both the bully's and the victim's reputation (Bouchrika,2024). Our present technological advancement age has significantly contributed to the bullying aspect of body. Body image issues due to self-comparison can lead to serious mental health concerns. Youth are also exposed to many mental health stressors like social comparison, fear of missing out, anxiety, depression etc. Thus, social media usage has a significant impact on mental wellbeing of youth. Mental wellbeing has deeper meaning and implication for our lives. It is how we respond to life's ups and downs. Mental wellbeing includes how a person thinks, handles emotion and acts (Bali, 2020). In a study among college students in Bangalore found that those who spent more time on social media showed lower mental well-being (Suchnadra, 2020). In a quality study among adolescents in U.K. showed that adolescents perceived social media as a threat to mental wellbeing. The participants found that it can cause anxiety and mood disorders. Social media platform becomes a space for cyberbullying and may leads to addiction (Reilley, 2018). Past literature found only very few studies which showed social media has a positive outcome in mental health among youth a (Schonning, 2020). The present study aimed to investigate the relationship between social media usage and mental well-being among youth. This study emphasizes on the dynamics of social media usage and its effect on mental health. Thus, it provides immense knowledge and further insights into developing healthier social media usage among youth. Study will help in promoting mental wellbeing in the digital world.

3. Methods:

3.1. Objective of Study: To identify the relationship among Social Media Usage and Mental Well-being among Young Adults.

3.2. Hypothesis of Study: There is significant relationship among Social Media Usage and Mental Well-being among Young Adults.

3.3. Tools Used:

> **Warwick Edinburgh Mental Well-being Scale (2008):** The Warwick-Edinburgh Mental Well-being Scale (WEMWBS) researchers at the Universities of Warwick and Edinburgh, with funding provided by NHS Health Scotland, to enable the measurement of mental well-being of adults in the UK. This scale measures mental well-being emphasing subjective well-being and psychological functioning and address different aspects of positive mental health. WEMWBS is a 14 item on a 1 to 5 Likert scale (1-None of the time to 5- All of the time). The internal consistency of the scale was measured using Cronbach's alpha coefficient which was in the acceptable range (0.93). The scale showed acceptable construct validity.

> **The Bergen Social Media Addiction Scale (Andreassen et al., 2016):** Bergen Social Media Addiction Scale is developed from the Bergen Facebook Addiction Scale. Bergen Facebook Addiction Scale (Andreassen et al., 2012) was developed with a student sample at the University of Bergen in Norway. The BSMAS assesses the difficulties an

individual faces due to social media's excessive usage and assess the severity accordingly. The six items of BSMAS are measured at a 5-point Likert scale ranging from 1 (very rarely) to 5 (very often).The BSMAS has shown good validity and reliability (Andreassen et al. 2016). The internal consistency of the BSMAS results high ($\alpha = 0.88$).

3.4. Procedure: A total of 154 sample were selected for the study. Participants were purposively selected from different districts of Kerala, age ranging from 18-25. Out of the 154 young adults, 95 are females and 59 males. The data collection was done using printed questionnaires and participants were provided with a consent form and a note on which details of the study were given. After giving consent, the participant can start doing the respective forms filling with the personal data sheet, through which the information regarding socio-demographic variables was collected. After filling up personal data sheet, the self-report inventories of Warwick-Edinburgh Mental Well-being Scale and **The Bergen Social Media Addiction Scale** were given to them. The collected data were analysed by using SPSS version 25 and the Spearman's Rank Correlation statistical technique was used in the study.

4. Result and Discussion:

Table 1: Interrelationship between   Social Media Usage and Mental Wellbeing (N=154).

Variables	Mental Wellbeing
Social Media Usage	-.247 *

* Correlation is significant at the 0.01 level (2-tailed)

A Spearman's Rho correlation test was sued to find the relationship between social media suage and mental wellbeing. The results of the correlation test is shown in table There is significant negative correlation between social media usage and mental wellbeing (r=-.247, p<0.01). The correlation r value -0.24 suggests a weak to moderate negative relationship. Findings showed that as social media usage increases, mental wellbeing tend to decrease among youth. This results also indicated that reduced social media usage will lead to higher mental wellbeing among youth. Thus, social media usage has a significant relationship with mental wellbeing. The present study was supported by Reilley (2018) qualitative research among 54 students in UK. The findings of the study showed that adolescents social media over usage act as a threat to mental wellbeing. The participants found that it can cause anxiety and mood disorders for some adolescents. Social media platform becomes a space for cyberbullying and may leads to addiction.

There are many reasons for the negative relationship between these study variables. It can be due to various social and psychological factors. Youth is after many social medias and their screen time is increasing over days such that binge watching reels and short videos ultimately lead to social comparison and relatively end to lower self-esteem. Social media makes space for self-comparison such that individuals compare oneself with others life style and gets disturbed. Such practices will diminish mental wellbeing among youth. In addition, social media engagement in many cases results in negative interactions. Cyber bullying and negative comments might dishearten individuals and affect their mental health. There are lot of negative news and reels which can affect the mental health of individuals across different age groups. Constant social media usage disrupts the daily routine of many people. It can reduce the sleep patterns and most often people lately go to bed. As young adults are in the growth phase adequate sleep and rest is essential for both physical and mental health. As screentime increases, it will also affect the eyes as it gets more stressed and it will lead to visual defects in future.

Social media usage reduces social interactions and people focus on more social media interactions. Thus, many peer group interactions and friendship get affected. Family discussions at home tend to diminished due to phone usage. People are addicted to social media such that their contents are so impressive and engaging. It has a very significant influence in their work productivity as if people spend more time on social media than for other engagements. Social media usage diminishes time for self-care routines and hobbies. People find less time for engaging in physical activities and exercises contributing to poor physical health.

This study provides insights about how social media usage relates to mental wellbeing. This is a technological era where the internet penetration is at its peak level. We cannot pause its use as it has all prevailing influence in our lives. But there are problems associated with overuse of smartphones and social media. Encouraging mindful social media habits. Findings from the present research can be used to explore the causal relationships in further research. Extending research to studying the positive outcomes from social media and finding ways for promoting mental wellbeing through social media will be effective. The present study is limited to young adults, it can be extended to other ages also, especially in case of old age people in order to explore the effects of social media usage in them. Awareness programs can be initiated in schools, colleges and organizations to provide knowledge in mental wellbeing and promoting offline interactions. Interventions can be developed to provide help in managing social media addiction.

5. Conclusion:

The study aims to identify the relationship among social media usage and mental well-being among young adults. In this technological era, the usage of social media is inevitable and but its usage has to be limited as if it has a direct relationship with mental wellbeing. Findings of the study reveal that both social media usage and mental wellbeing have a significant negative correlation. Thus, the study provides insights about how social media usage relates to mental wellbeing. Further studies should investigate the predictors of overuse of social media and causal relationship has to be explored.

References:

1. Andreassen, C. S., Torsheim, T., Brunborg, G. S., and Pallesen, S. (2012). Development of a Facebook addiction scale. *Psychological Reports, 110*(2), 501-517. https://doi.org/10.2466/02.09.PR0.110.2.501-517

2. Bouchrika, I. (2024). Teenage cyberbullying statistics: Prevalence and impact of social media. *Research.com.* https://research.com/education/teenage-cyberbullying-statistics

3. Diga, M., and Kelleher, T. (2009). Social media use, perceptions of decision-making power, and public roles. *Public Relations Review, 35*(4), 440-442. https://doi.org/10.1016/j.pubrev.2009.07.003

4. Kaplan, A. M., and Haenlein, M. (2010). Users of the world, unite: The challenges and opportunities of social media. *Business Horizons, 53*(1), 59-68. https://doi.org/10.1016/j.bushor.2009.09.003

5. Bali, M. K. (2020). Mental well-being in polyamorous and monogamous relationships. *International Journal of Indian Psychology, 8*(3), 316-327. https://doi.org/10.25215/0803.039

6. O'Reilly, I. (1970). Social media and its associations with body satisfaction, exercise, and eating habits in undergraduate students. *DBS eSource Home.* https://esource.dbs.ie/handle/10788/3466

7. Petrosyan, A. (2024). Statista report. *Statista.* https://www.statista.com/statistics/617136/digital-population-worldwide/

8. Shanhong, L. (2020). Statista report Nokia 2020. *Statista.* https://www.statista.com/statistics/278414/number-of-worldwide-social-network-users/

9. Suchandra, G. (2020). The effect of social media usage on the mental well-being of medical college students in Bangalore, Karnataka. *PubMed Central.* https://www.ncbi.nlm.nih.gov/pmc/articles/PMC7842463/

10. Tennant, R., Hiller, L., and Fishwick, R. (2007). The Warwick-Edinburgh Mental Well-being Scale (WEMWBS): Development and UK validation. *Health Quality Life Outcomes, 5,* 63. https://doi.org/10.1186/1477-7525-5-63

5. PSYCHOLOGICAL IMPACTS OF SOCIAL MEDIA ON YOUTH

Ekatrika Ghosh[1], Dr. Papia Mukherjee[2]*

[1]Ph.D Scholar, Department of Psychology, Swami Vivekananda University,

[2]*Assistant Professor, Department of psychology, Swami Vivekananda University

Email: **papiam@svu.ac.in**

Abstract:

The purpose of this chapter is to investigate the multifaceted psychological consequences that social media platforms have on the mental health and well-being of young people, a group that is especially susceptible to the effects of digital connectedness. This study, which draws on recent research, investigates the ways in which social media platforms such as Instagram, TikTok, and Snapchat have an impact on individuals' self-esteem, body image, social comparison, and emotional regulation. In this chapter, both good and negative results are discussed. These outcomes include improved emotions of social connectivity and validation, as well as the dangers of anxiety, despair, and loneliness that may occur as a result of cyberbullying, online harassment, and unattainable standards of success or attractiveness. Additionally, it discusses the role that parental supervision, media literacy, and measures for digital detoxification have in minimizing the negative impacts of technology. In the end, the chapter underlines the need of taking a balanced approach to the usage of social media by supporting digital wellness practices that foster positive connections online while also protecting mental health.

Keywords: Social media, Psychological Impact, Social Comparison, Youth, mental health, Well-being, Social Connectivity

1. Introduction:

Social media is a kind of mass media communication on the Internet, including platforms for social networking and microblogging, where people exchange information, ideas, personal messages, and other material, such as videos. Social networking and social media are interconnected ideas; however, social networking often refers to individuals forming groups, while social media focuses on using social networking sites and other platforms to cultivate an audience.Social media is a category of mass media communication on the Internet, including platforms for social networking and microblogging, where users disseminate information, ideas, personal messages, and other material, including videos. Social networking and social media are interconnected ideas; however, social networking often refers to individuals forming groups, while social media focuses on using social networking sites and other platforms to cultivate an audience.

2. Social Media Usage and Youth:

The information accessed by children and teens online has emerged as a contemporary issue that requires prompt resolution. The poll addresses several facets about inclination, patterns, susceptibility, and awareness associated with internet use. A majority of Indian youth, including 85% of non-adult users, has access to cellphones. The majority engage online for five hours daily, with 80% acknowledging their use of social media. An increasing percentage of young individuals are viewing videos on OTT platforms other than YouTube. Nonetheless, there exists a deficiency in understanding about privacy and safety control mechanisms on internet platforms. Approximately 30% of respondents acknowledged sharing sensitive information online, while 50% confessed to seeing online pornography, and 40% confirmed knowing others who had accessed pornographic material on the internet.

During the lockdown period of June to July 2020, the survey URLs were sent over many social media platforms, resulting in 1154 legitimate replies being used. The all-India survey included North East India. The highest number of answers came from Maharashtra, followed by Uttar Pradesh and Rajasthan. According to the sample, female respondents constituted 48%, male respondents 51%, and 1% identified as other. The poll focused on the historical context of internet use and its daily length. The majority of young responders use the internet via their smartphones. According to the study, the majority of young users acknowledged using the internet mostly for socializing with friends or utilizing social media sites. Individuals of all age demographics are using the internet for educational, professional, social, and recreational activities. Instagram is the predominant social media site for the 18-25 age group, whilst Facebook is favored by those aged 25-40 and 40 and beyond.

3. Positive Effects on Youth:

Even though a lot of the conversation about social media highlights its downsides, there are actually some positive effects that these platforms can have on young people. Social media can help build important connections, offer learning opportunities, and support personal development in different ways. There are several important positive effects to consider:

a) **Social Connectivity and Support Networks:** social media helps young people connect with friends, family, and others around the world, which is important for building and keeping relationships. For people in isolated or marginalized communities, these platforms can provide a sense of belonging and support, helping to lessen feelings of loneliness and alienation.

b) **Improved Learning and Creativity:** Sites such as YouTube, TikTok, and Instagram offer a ton of educational videos, tutorials, and opportunities for creative expression. Young people can connect with content that matches their interests, learn new skills, and explore hobbies like photography, writing, coding, or art. This helps to boost creativity and promotes continuous learning throughout life.

c) **Awareness:** Social media helps young people become more aware of social and political issues and encourages them to advocate for change. It offers a space for young people to share their thoughts, support social issues, and get involved in activism. By being exposed to different viewpoints and movements, young people can build a better understanding of social responsibility and help create positive change.

d) **Identity:** Social media gives young people a chance to figure out who they are, what they like, and what matters to them in ways that might be hard to do in real life. Social media can really help with figuring out who you are and expressing yourself. You can try out different styles, share your own stories, and connect with people who think like you.

e) **Support:** Youth often turn to social media to find mental health resources, discover coping strategies, and connect with peers for support. Online communities and influencers that focus on mental health awareness can really help by sharing important information and reducing stigma. This encourages young people to talk about their feelings, seek help, and feel less alone in what they're going through.

f) **Connection:** Social media platforms such as LinkedIn and Twitter provide chances for young people to connect, establish professional relationships, and investigate different career options. Social media is a great tool for those looking to promote themselves, connect with professionals in their field, and create a personal brand. Engaging with different perspectives and communities on social media can really help young people build empathy and emotional intelligence. It helps them to grasp different perspectives, acknowledge their feelings, and work on communicating well in both online and face-to-face situations. To sum up, even though social media has its challenges, it also offers a lot of opportunities for personal growth, building social connections, and learning for young people. By encouraging good online experiences and building digital skills, young people can take advantage of social media in ways that help them grow and feel good about themselves.

4. Negative Effects on Youth:

Even though there can be some good effects, social media can also bring about a lot of negative impacts on young people, particularly because they are still growing emotionally and psychologically. The effects can really influence mental health, self-esteem, social relationships, and overall well-being. Here are a few important negative effects to consider:

a). Cyberbullying and Digital Harassment: Cyberbullying and online harassment are defined as deliberate and recurrent damage inflicted using technology, including text messaging applications, social media platforms, or the internet. It encompasses humiliation, embarrassment, extortion, or intimidation. Individuals subjected to cyberbullying may encounter several mental health challenges, including isolation, sadness, social anxiety, and self-harm. In severe or extended instances of this kind of bullying, it may lead to suicidal ideation or actions. Research on adolescents and social media reveals alarming statistics—approximately 46% of teenagers in the United States have encountered at least one instance of cyberbullying, while 28% have experienced many incidents. Additional startling discoveries encompass:

- ➢ 32% report having been labelled with derogatory names.
- ➢ 22% have experienced the dissemination of rumours about them.
- ➢ 17% have gotten unsolicited sexual photographs.
- ➢ 15% describe persistent inquiries about their location, activities, or companions.
- ➢ 10% have experienced violent threats.
- ➢ 7% indicate that explicit pictures of themselves have been disseminated without authorization.

In a study done by Mitch Van Geel et al., 2017 it was found that Agreeableness, Machiavellianism, and psychopathy are predictors of conventional bullying, Agreeableness is a predictor of cyberbullying. It was also found that Sadism is a predictor of conventional bullying when controlling for Dark Triad features. In another study it was It was also shown that an under controlled personality predisposes adolescents to widespread involvement in cyberbullying (AinzaraFavini et al., 2023)

b). Body Image Issues: Social media significantly influences body image, shaping individuals' perceptions of their own bodies and those of others. It can serve as a catalyst for empowerment and body positivity for some, while simultaneously fostering body dissatisfaction and promoting unhealthy beauty standards for others. Below is an analysis of the effects of social media on body image.

Social media sites such as Instagram, TikTok, and Snapchat often display meticulously selected photographs in which individuals only share their most favorable events. Filters, editing applications, and Photoshop may fabricate a false standard of beauty, wherein features and bodies are refined, elongated, or augmented in manners that do not accurately reflect reality. Influencers, models, and celebrities often embody an idealized physique, which might exert pressure on people to conform to that standard. These criteria may differ, although often prioritize certain body proportions (such as slenderness or hourglass silhouettes) or distinct skin tones, facial attributes, and hair textures that may not accurately reflect the diversity of all humans.

A significant proportion of teenager grapple with body image issues, particularly females (Daniels et al., 2020; Neumark-Sztainer et al., 2006). Concerns may include body dissatisfaction and weight/shape issues (Thompson et al., 1999), body shame (McKinley and Hyde 1996), and self-objectification (Fredrickson and Roberts 1997). A recent nationally representative study of U.S. adolescents and young adults aged 14-24 revealed that worries around weight and body shape intensified during the COVID-19 pandemic, with 40% of participants indicating they had engaged in actions to regulate their weight and/or shape during this period (Schmid et al. 2022).

c). Porn Addiction: In recent years, there has been a lot of talk about two distinct but often related behavioral issues: porn addiction and social media addiction. They are both linked to the impact that digital media has on people's attention spans, emotional well-being, and behavioral patterns. Here we take a look at the individual effects of porn addiction and the ways in which social media may amplify those effects. There are physical, social, and mental health issues that may arise from an addiction to porn and social media. Effects on Mental Health: Anxiety, sadness, and other mood problems are more common in those who suffer from both addictions. Anxieties about social comparison, inadequacy, and loneliness may worsen with a porn addiction, whereas shame, guilt, and emotional numbness can accompany social media addiction.

c) Dopamine Deregulation: When people spend too much time on pornographic websites and social media, it may mess with their brain's reward system, making it so they need more and more of the activity to have the same impact, and then they start to feel sick when they don't have any of it. The social impact of both addictions is the pressure they put on personal relationships. Addiction to porn may damage relationships by eroding trust, intimacy, and connection, while social media addiction can lead to resentment, miscommunication, or neglect.

d) Isolation: People who are addicted to social media may experience what is known as "digital isolation," in which they rely on their online connections more than their actual contacts with others. When people get addicted to porn, they may stop seeking out good, close connections, which may lead to a feeling of emotional remoteness.

Addiction to porn may have the same escalating behavioural impact as an addiction to social media, leading users to squander hours in repeated activities that take them away from their personal, professional, and social obligations.

e) Irrational Expectations: Both addictions may lead to distorted thinking. The idealized or edited lives shown on social media might cloud one's view of the world. Similarly, pornographic media often presents sex in an unrealistic or exaggerated light, which may influence viewers to have skewed views of sexuality, body image, and intimacy. In a study it was found that Pornography exposure is negatively associated with body image (Paslakis et al., 2022). One possible consequence is that pornographic material on social media can lead some users to finally stop viewing porn (Martini et al., 2023)

d) Stress: In this digital era, the effects of stress and addiction to social media on young people are becoming more and more of a worry. Particularly for young people (those between the ages of 18 and 29), who are still maturing into their identities, coping strategies, and social abilities, these two elements may have a major impact on their psychological, emotional, and social health. Let's take a look at how these two problems might influence young people: An increasing worry in this digital era is the effect of stress and addiction to social media on young people. Adolescents and young adults, who are still learning to cope, are more vulnerable to the negative effects of these two elements on their psychological, emotional, and social health. A young person's capacity to concentrate on long-term objectives, academics, or even face-to-face interactions may be diminished due to the continual diversions and instant satisfaction offered by social media.Social media's "likes" and comments provide users with brief moments of approval or enjoyment, which might make it harder for them to wait their turn or persevere when faced with obstacles.systems, personal identity, and interpersonal abilities. Isolation and lack of social connection are common symptoms of stress among young people, which may lead them to retreat from their social networks.

In a study it was found that among young people, social media had no discernible effect on stress levels. The interaction was entirely mediated by fatalism instead (Ngien et al,2022). Research has shown that social media addiction (SMA) is a predictor of stress linked to peer neglect (Fabris et al., 2020).

e). Fear of Missing Out: When it comes to young people, there is a strong correlation between social media addiction and FOMO, which may lead to a cascade of emotional, mental, and social problems. Now we'll take a look at how fear of missing out (FOMO) affects social media use and how this vicious cycle might have bad outcomes. The fear of missing out (FOMO) is the concern that one will not be able to participate in an enjoyable or significant activity that other people are taking part in. In the context of social media, it shows up when people feel inadequate or left out when they see postings from famous people, influencers, or friends doing things like going on vacation or reaching a milestone. Everywhere you look, there's an update about some social event, party, hangout, or gathering on social media. If someone is already susceptible to FOMO, this can make them feel even more alone. This anxiety may cause individuals to increase their social media use in the vain hope that they will see an invitation or post about an event that they may be able to attend. Everywhere you look, there's an update about some social event, party, hangout, or gathering on social media. If someone is already susceptible to FOMO, this can make them feel even more alone. This anxiety may cause individuals to increase their social media use in the vain hope that they will see an invitation or post about an event that they may be able to attend. In a study it was shown that FOMO was positively correlated with social media addiction (Bakioglu et al., 2022). A significant correlation was found between social media addiction and Fear of missing out (Setyaningsih et al., 2023) social media addiction was found to be positively and directly correlated with fear of missing out (Hamutoglu, 2020)

h). Anxiety: Pressures from online comparison, validation-seeking, and social dynamics may have a disproportionately negative effect on young adults and adolescents, making them more vulnerable to the anxiety-inducing effects of social media. Although there are some great sides of social media, including connecting with others, receiving encouragement, and expressing oneself, it may also have a large and sometimes overwhelming negative impact on anxiety. Now that we've shown that social media may have an effect on anxiety, let's examine how this effect occurs and what we can do to lessen it. The Link Between Social Anxiety and Online Platforms The vast and ever-expanding realm of social media consists of interconnected websites that enable users to instantaneously share content with their entire buddy network. It didn't take long for these sites to gain massive popularity; now, billions of people use them daily. These interactive platforms are driving a dramatic increase in social anxiety, despite the seemingly innocent nature of such services. A lot of people's mental health is taking a hit because of these social networks. There are an increasing number of factors in today's society that are associated with social media, and over fifteen million Americans have been diagnosed with social anxiety. Although the ages range greatly, the majority of these instances begin in people as young as thirteen.

Social media addiction was found to be correlated with anxiety (BKeles et al ,2020).Significant predictors of burnout were addiction, jealousy, and anxiety related to social media usage (Chang Liu et al,2020)

i). Depression: Based on study that was published by the American Psychological Association (APA), it has been shown that children who spend more time addicted to screens and less time playing outdoors, exercising, and connecting with others are at an elevated risk for developing symptoms of depression. According to the findings of the study, the likelihood of youngsters experiencing better levels of happiness is increased when they participate in a greater number of activities that do not require the use of screens. When it comes to adolescents, the chance of receiving a diagnosis of social media depression is increased by a factor of two when they spend five hours per day on the internet and social media. Depression brought on by social media might begin when a young person experiences feelings of inadequacy in their online social groups. Participation in social media was shown to have a positive correlation with signs of depression. Haand et al., 2020 studied According to the findings of another research (Kircaburun et al., 2016), it was clear that addiction to social media was having an indirect impact as well.

5. Conclusion:

The conclusion is that social media has become an essential component of the culture of young people, and it has the ability to impact the lives of young people in both good and harmful ways.

On the bright side, social media platforms provide opportunities for self-expression, social connection, and access to educational materials. These platforms enable young people to broaden their social networks, participate in artistic activities, and receive exposure to a variety of viewpoints. It also has the potential to serve as a tool for activism, making it possible for young people to become involved in social causes and to bring attention to significant problems. On the other hand, the influence of social media is not devoid of difficulties altogether. It is possible that difficulties such as body image worries, anxiety, sadness, and loneliness might be exacerbated by the frequent exposure to idealized pictures, peer comparisons, and the pressure to maintain a specific online identity. In addition, the addictive quality of social media, together with its algorithms that are meant to attract attention, often results in a reduction in face-to-face contacts and a disruption of sleep habits, both of which may have a severe impact on an individual's overall psychological and physiological health. The pressure that young people feel to acquire validation via likes, shares, and follows may also skew the way that they evaluate their own sense of self-worth. Additionally, the emergence of cyberbullying has brought new types of damage that were not as prominent before the advent of the digital era. In addition, the dissemination of false information on social media platforms poses a barrier to the process of developing people who are knowledgeable and capable of critical thinking. When it comes down to it, the influence of social media on young people is complicated and multi-faceted. It is essential for educators, parents, and politicians to help young people in utilizing these platforms in a healthy and productive manner. It presents both possibilities and hazards, and it is essential that they get guidance in this regard. Fostering media literacy, supporting digital well-being, and encouraging open talks about the issues of social media usage will be vital in the future in order to assist young people in learning how to navigate the digital world in a responsible and aware manner.

Reference:

1. Bakioğlu, F., Deniz, M., Griffiths, M. D., & Pakpour, A. H. (2022). Adaptation and validation of the Online-Fear of Missing Out Inventory into Turkish and the association with social media addiction, smartphone addiction, and life satisfaction. *BMC Psychology, 10*(1), 154. https://doi.org/10.1186/s40359-022-00816-3

2. Daniels, E. A., Zurbriggen, E. L., & Ward, L. M. (2020). Becoming an object: A review of self-objectification in girls. *Body Image, 33,* 278-299. https://doi.org/10.1016/j.bodyim.2020.06.003

3. Favini, A., Gerbino, M., Pastorelli, C., Zuffiano, A., Lunetti, C., Remondi, C., ... & Giannini, A. M. (2023). Bullying and cyberbullying: Do personality profiles matter in adolescence?. *Telematics and Informatics Reports, 12,* 100108. https://doi.org/10.1016/j.tele.2023.100108

4. Fabris, M. A., Marengo, D., Longobardi, C., & Settanni, M. (2020). Investigating the links between fear of missing out, social media addiction, and emotional symptoms in adolescence: The role of stress associated with neglect and negative reactions on social media. *Addictive Behaviors, 106,* 106364. https://doi.org/10.1016/j.addbeh.2020.106364

5. Fredrickson, B. L., & Roberts, T. A. (1997). Objectification theory: Toward understanding women's lived experiences and mental health risks. *Psychology of Women Quarterly, 21*(2), 173-206. https://doi.org/10.1111/j.1471-6402.1997.tb00108.x

6. Haand, R., & Shuwang, Z. (2020). The relationship between social media addiction and depression: A quantitative study among university students in Khost, Afghanistan. *International Journal of Adolescence and Youth, 25*(1), 780-786. https://doi.org/10.1080/02673843.2019.1626193

7. Keles, B., McCrae, N., & Grealish, A. (2020). A systematic review: The influence of social media on depression, anxiety, and psychological distress in adolescents. *International Journal of Adolescence and Youth, 25*(1), 79-93. https://doi.org/10.1080/02673843.2019.1638013

8. Kircaburun, K. (2016). Self-esteem, daily internet use, and social media addiction as predictors of depression among Turkish adolescents. *Journal of Education and Practice, 7*(24), 64-72. https://www.iiste.org/Journals/index.php/JEP/article/view/33471

9. Liu, C., & Ma, J. (2020). Social media addiction and burnout: The mediating roles of envy and social media use anxiety. *Current Psychology, 39*(6), 1883-1891. https://doi.org/10.1007/s12144-019-00315-1

10. Martini, D., & Gangadharbatla, H. (2023). Pornified content on social media: Exploring the impact on Brazilian addicts. *The Journal of Social Media in Society, 12*(1), 257-285. https://www.thejsms.org/

11. McKinley, N. M. (1998). Gender differences in undergraduates' body esteem: The mediating effect of objectified body consciousness and actual/ideal weight discrepancy. *Sex Roles, 39*(1), 113-123. https://doi.org/10.1023/A:1018760625757

12. Ngien, A., & Jiang, S. (2022). The effect of social media on stress among young adults during the COVID-19 pandemic: Taking into account fatalism and social media exhaustion. *Health Communication, 37*(10), 1337-1344. https://doi.org/10.1080/10410236.2022.2043245

13. Neumark-Sztainer, D., Levine, M. P., Paxton, S. J., Smolak, L., Piran, N., & Wertheim, E. H. (2006). Prevention of body dissatisfaction and disordered eating: What next?. *Eating Disorders, 14*(4), 265-285. https://doi.org/10.1080/10640260600825841

14. Paslakis, G., Chiclana Actis, C., & Mestre-Bach, G. (2022). Associations between pornography exposure, body image, and sexual body image: A systematic review. *Journal of Health Psychology, 27*(3), 743-760. https://doi.org/10.1177/13591053221103362

15. Setyaningsih, N., Sarjana, W., & Wardani, N. D. (2023). The correlation between fear of missing out (FoMO) and internet addiction in vocational high school students. *Surabaya Psychiatry Journal/Jurnal Psikiatri Surabaya, 12*(1). https://doi.org/10.30829/jps.12.1.2023.10058

16. Schmid, J. C., Rose, K. L., Hadler, N. L., Amaro, X., Frank, A., Wilkie, E., ... & Sonneville, K. R. (2022). Content analysis of the impact of COVID-19 on weight and shape control behaviors and social media content of US adolescents and young adults. *Eating Behaviors, 45*, 101635. https://doi.org/10.1016/j.eatbeh.2022.101635

17. Thompson, J. K., Coovert, M. D., & Stormer, S. M. (1999). Body image, social comparison, and eating disturbance: A covariance structure modeling investigation. *International Journal of Eating Disorders, 26*(1), 43-51. https://doi.org/10.1002/(SICI)1098-108X(199907)26:1<43::AID-EAT4>3.0.CO;2-6

18. van Geel, M., Goemans, A., Toprak, F., & Vedder, P. (2017). Which personality traits are related to traditional bullying and cyberbullying? A study with the Big Five, Dark Triad, and sadism. *Personality and Individual Differences, 106*, 231-235. https://doi.org/10.1016/j.paid.2016.10.047

6. CULTURAL PRACTICES AND SOCIAL CHANGE IN CONTEMPORARY SOCIETIES

Sunanda Das

Ph. D. Research Scholar, Tata Institute of Social Sciences, Hyderabad

Email: hp2020ss008@stud.tiss.edu

Abstract:

The concept of "God" is deeply subjective, as people have different understandings and representations of the divine, seeing "black gods," "pink gods," and "white gods." This highlights the diverse ways humans interact with and interpret the world around them. Culture, as defined here, refers to the human-made aspects of the environment, including education, sports, leisure, archaeology, history, aesthetics, and architecture. Recent developments within aesthetics have shown a growing sensitivity to the social and folk contexts in which art is both produced and consumed. Contemporary and postmodern art have increasingly reflected on their own status as art forms. Marxist theory uses the metaphor of architecture to describe the relationship between the economy and society: just as the size and structure of a building depend on its foundations, the characteristics of non-economic spheres of human life depend on the nature of economic activity. According to Marxism, the economic base is composed of the forces and relations of production. Cultural anthropology seeks to explain the generation of meaning through the relationship between mutually exclusive terms, forming a system of oppositions, such as culture/nature, dark/light, and male/female. This study's paradigm shift involves exploring the intersection of subcultures, race, gender, literary criticism, popular culture, and mass media.

Keywords: French Revolution, Industrial Revolution, race, gender, popular culture, aesthetics.

1. Introduction:

The concept of the body in national education systems grows through the development of a sense of place. A semiotic approach can be applied to the body, interpreting it through the lens of meaning. The body is not merely an instinctive element of nature, but rather it is intertwined with philosophical and cultural frameworks (Geertz, 1973). It serves as a significant site where culture and national identity are expressed, often through clothing, jewelry, and other forms of adornment, as well as through the regulation of bodily forms, such as hairdos and physical appearance. These practices of body modification and presentation are indicative of deeper cultural meanings (Sahlins, 1976).

The development of symbolism in the industrial context follows the theoretical framework established by Levi-Strauss's work in physical anthropology (Levi-Strauss, 1966). The French term *bricoleur* refers to a type of worker skilled in reassembling or repurposing various materials for new uses, often improvising and creating innovative ways to utilize items. In cultural theory, the term extends to the process by which elements of mainstream culture are appropriated and transformed by subcultures. This can include using language, fashion, or behavior in ways that challenge and subvert dominant ideologies (Geertz, 1973).

Anthropology, which broadly examines humanity and human culture, is divided into two main branches: physical (biological) and cultural anthropology. Physical anthropology focuses on the biological diversity within human populations and the study of human evolution. In the 19th century, this field was often used to justify the superiority of white European cultures over others, with racial differences described in evolutionary terms (Sahlins, 1976).

However, contemporary physical anthropology now emphasizes human diversity in relation to different environmental contexts. A similar transformation occurred in cultural anthropology, which emerged as a respected social science in the early 20th century. The early focus on the development of human civilization and philosophy shifted toward recognizing the diversity of human cultures, the complex systems that shape them, and the factors that sustain these cultural practices (Levi-Strauss, 1966).

2. Theoretical Framework:

Some of the most significant anthropologists, particularly in the contemporary development of the discipline, include Marcel Mauss and Franz Boas. Mauss, the nephew and student of Émile Durkheim, developed a comparative method for anthropology. Through ethnographic data, his theories sought to detect common patterns in the organization of social life. In *The Gift* (1966), Mauss studies the concept of gift exchange. He argued that the talent involved in gifting carries a joint moral duty. The gift must be repaid, in some way, at a later date. Gift exchange, therefore, can be seen as an "overall shared fact," a force that operates throughout society in economic, legal, political, and spiritual domains. Political power may thus be maintained through a leader's ability to offer gifts, compelling recipients to repay the gift with political loyalty. While Mauss contributed to the theoretical side of anthropology, emphasizing the difficulty of other philosophies and the cognitive aspects of culture, he also provided a framework for understanding how these social practices worked (Mauss, 1963).

Franz Boas, on the other hand, advocated for the empirical side of anthropology. Boas stressed the importance of studying the everyday life of cultures, arguing that the significance of research and ethnographic techniques lay in their ability to uncover the nuances of social life within a culture. His approach focused on empirical data and detailed observation (Boas, 1940).

Bronislaw Malinowski's study of the Trobriand Islanders of New Guinea (1922) provided a model for rigorous anthropological research for many years. It combined meticulous ethnographic descriptions of the society with a functionalist explanatory framework. Malinowski sought to explain various features and institutions of the society in terms of the functions they fulfilled, that is, the needs they satisfied in order to maintain and reproduce the culture. The functionalist approach dominated anthropology prior to World War II, with British anthropologists such as E.E. Evans-Pritchard (1951) and A.R. Radcliffe-Brown (1952) playing prominent roles. Meanwhile, in the United States, Ruth Benedict and Margaret Mead (1928) carried out important work. Benedict's (1935) research produced remarkably elegant interpretations of cultures through dominant themes. For instance, Japanese culture is seen to balance two themes: "sword" and "chrysanthemum." In the nature versus nurture debate, Benedict suggested that factors like cultural acquisition and genetic inheritance play significant roles in shaping human personality and traits. At the extreme, her work implied that a newborn human could be seen as a "blank slate" upon which culture could inscribe whatever traits it wished, highlighting the importance of socialization (Benedict, 1935).

The work of Mauss and Radcliffe-Brown significantly influenced Claude Lévi-Strauss and the development of structuralist anthropology in the immediate post-war period. His *Elementary Structures of Kinship* (1969) examined marriage rules in the manner of Mauss's "total social fact." For example, the widespread custom of preferring first cousins as spouses was seen as essential for ensuring meaningful exchanges between male-dominated clans. Women were considered the "message" passed between clans, as they give away daughters and receive wives. Lévi-Strauss's work was also influenced by Ferdinand de Saussure's semiology and Radcliffe-Brown's studies of mythological structures, particularly the use of binary oppositions in articulating the meanings of myths. In *Mythologiques* (1970, 1973, 1978, 1981) and *The Savage Mind* (1966), Lévi-Strauss explored not only how human cultures organize classificatory systems but also how these systems integrate their understanding of the natural world with their social world. He argued that the diversity of particular mythologies and beliefs can be understood as employing a limited set of meaningful units or symbols. The combination of these elements is governed by rules that resemble grammatical transformations. Myths, Lévi-Strauss suggested, operate within an underlying structure akin to Saussure's *langue*, while the surface-level expressions of myths are akin to *parole* (Lévi-Strauss, 1966, 1970, 1973, 1978, 1981).

At a less extreme position, cultural anthropology continues to recognize the diversity and validity of other cultures as cognitive systems. This has led to the emergence of subdisciplines within cultural anthropology, such as ethnomedicine, which studies how non-Western cultures organize and articulate their knowledge of medicine (Good, 1993).

3. Cultural Capital:

Class involvement is distinct, at least within the Marxist tradition, in terms of a person's access to and control of economic wealth (such as manufacturing equipment, raw resources, and money). Pierre Bourdieu (1973) drew an analogy between a person's access to national capital and the role of educational institutions in a market-driven, entrepreneurial society. Children require varying levels of social competence learned before university, typically within the home. The educational system does not openly distinguish based on the class of the children. Instead, all children are measured "neutrally" in terms of their ability to perform according to the same standards of excellence. These standards, however, are shaped by the dominant class. Children from the dominant class tend to perform better, benefiting from the symbolic power associated with their parents' access to national capital.

4. Cultural Relativism:

The view that fundamentally different standards of morality, practices, and belief systems operate in different cultures and cannot be judged with regard to their worth from a standpoint exterior to them is known as cultural relativism. Cultural relativism holds that there is a fundamental incommensurability between the value systems of different cultures (Herskovits, 1958). Whether or not such a view commits one to relativism with regard to questions of knowledge is another issue, which depends on whether or not one is inclined to hold that the rules of validity that apply to the construction of knowledge claims are culturally constructed (Geertz, 1973). However, it is difficult to see how a cultural relativist can defend any notion of epistemic validity from the charge of being likewise culturally produced and, therefore, incommensurable with conceptions of validity that are generated within different cultures or contexts (Nagel, 1986). It is possible to define more recent cultural relativism in terms of its commitment to a particular model of language and meaning derived from the work of the later Wittgenstein (Wittgenstein, 1953).

5. Cultural Reproduction:

The term "cultural reproduction" was introduced by Pierre Bourdieu (1973) to refer to the process by which the philosophy, and thus political control, of the dominant class is maintained from one generation to the next, through the educational system. More generally, the term can be understood to highlight the problem of how cultures continue to persist and remain relatively unchanged over long periods of time. This continued existence requires more than just neutral physical reproduction, in the sense of adequate labor to replace individuals who have died or left the culture. The philosophy of that culture must be communicated to the new generation. National reproduction is thus closely linked to the role that socialization, or the process through which individuals acquire the norms of their societies, plays in this stability. According to Bourdieu's framework, part of this issue of cultural reproduction is not just the persistence of the core values and politics of a culture, but rather the persistence of political structures and the structures of power and domination within society. In this way, cultural reproduction can be understood as a process by which political structures are legitimized or normalized. National education reproduces ethnography, fictional criticism, sociobiology, aesthetics, race, class, gender, production and consumption, and semiotics.

6. Cultural Industry:

Adorno's critique of the culture industry is one of the significant theories within Western Marxism. It argues that while individuals shape knowledge, the culture industry shapes individuals. The process of realization is increasingly lost, and the general cultural quality of society becomes superficial. Under the influence of the culture industry, individual creativity is continuously reduced, and, ultimately, philosophy cannot produce true enlightenment (Adorno & Horkheimer, 1972). However, the culture industry is not without value. We must recognize both the positive and negative aspects of the culture industry through a dialectical and critical analysis, and appropriately interpret the nature of this dangerous philosophy by examining the structure of the culture industry itself. The culture industry reproduces notions of the cosmos, culture, and humanity, and modern industrial societies increasingly attempt to address the emotional and artistic needs of the public. Although cultural products differ in substantial ways, once they enter the market, they are no longer pure forms of art but become commodified products (Adorno & Horkheimer, 1972). The purpose of cultural production is to fulfill the spiritual and cultural needs of the public, and its primary value is imagination. The rise of the culture industry aims to meet the public's mystical needs. However, once cultural products are created, their goal is no longer to serve the public but to accumulate wealth. Thus, the ultimate goal of the culture industry is to create exchange value, with its focus consistently placed on exchange value rather than use value, which emphasizes humanistic care and life itself (Adorno, 1975). Adorno argues that the culture industry deteriorates the critical faculties and the autonomy of consumers. The culture industry may appear prosperous, but in reality, it limits the development of general philosophy and restricts artistic judgment (Adorno & Horkheimer, 1972). Simultaneously, he asserts that philosophy and art are commodified. Product fetishism endures in capitalist society. Regarding Adorno's critique of the culture industry, in contemporary China, it is neither entirely negative nor entirely positive, and it should be examined realistically in conjunction with the specific context of the nation. Adorno's enduring critique of the culture industry has historical roots. Moreover, as the culture industry has flourished in capitalist society, it is essential to critically examine the spirit of the culture industry. This is of significant importance for the development of China's cultural industry today (Zhang, 2020).

7. Cultural Practices and Subculture:

A subgroup is often misunderstood; it refers to a smaller collective within a larger society. People in a subgroup are part of the larger society but also possess unique characteristics that distinguish them from the mainstream. In the United States, there are thousands of subgroups. Cultural and ethnic groups share elements of their heritage, including language, food, and customs. Other subgroups are united by shared experiences. For example, biker culture revolves around a devotion to motorcycles, while certain subgroups are formed by individuals who possess interests or traits that differ from those of the general population. This can include artistic expressions related to body modification, such as tattoos, piercings, and other forms of physical alteration. In the United States, youth often form subgroups to cultivate a distinct adolescent identity. Alcoholics Anonymous provides support for individuals suffering from alcoholism. Although members of a subgroup may bond closely, they remain part of the larger society. Sociologists distinguish subgroups from countercultures, which are types of subgroups that reject certain values or ethics of the larger culture. Unlike mainstream cultures, which tend to integrate smoothly into society, countercultures actively challenge the dominant values and norms, sometimes even creating alternative communities outside of mainstream society (Hebdige, 1979).

Fads, a term used for movements following popular trends, can also be considered a type of counterculture. For example, the "Yearning for Zion" (YFZ) group in Eldorado, Texas, existed outside the norm and attracted attention when its leader was accused of child sexual abuse and underage marriage. The group's beliefs clashed so strongly with U.S. law that in 2008, authorities raided their compound, removing over 200 women and children (Bakker, 2009). Similarly, the American hipster is a well-known figure in modern society. Predominantly based in urban areas, especially in neighborhoods like Williamsburg in New York City, hipsters define themselves through a rejection of mainstream values. As a subgroup, hipsters embrace vintage fashion, nonconformity, and a resistance to authority and wealth. Although the hipster movement may seem like a recent trend among the younger bourgeoisie, its roots date back to the early 1900s.

Where did the hipster philosophy originate? In the early 1940s, jazz music was on the rise in the United States. Jazz bands were known for their "hepcat" members, who embodied a relaxed, unconventional lifestyle that defied social norms (Murray, 2010). People who were "hep" or "hip" followed their own codes, often using unique slang. The term "hipster" emerged organically as part of this subculture. In the jazz scene, saying "It's cool, man" did not simply mean that everything was fine; it conveyed a sense of acceptance of life as it was, without judgment (Giro, 2008).

8. Conclusion:

Cultural practices and societal change are deeply interconnected, with each influencing and shaping the other. Change, whether positive or negative, can have significant impacts on a culture, especially in the wake of major societal shifts. After the French and Industrial Revolutions, dramatic changes occurred in the class system, roles, power structures, laws, religion, ideology, and the very fabric of human reality. These revolutions led to the dismantling of traditional systems such as the estates and guild structures, fundamentally altering how societies were organized and how individuals interacted within those systems. The cultural shift that accompanied these changes was profound, reshaping not just political structures but also cultural norms and values. The role of sociology, as observed by scholars, is to elevate understanding beyond surface-level knowledge, providing deeper insights into these transformations and the ways they shape modern societies. Cultural practices, in turn, both reflect and propel societal change, emphasizing the importance of studying the dynamics between culture, power, and transformation to fully understand the evolution of societies.

References:

1. Adorno, T. W. (1975). *Introduction to the sociology of music.* Seabury Press.

2. Adorno, T. W., & Horkheimer, M. (1972). *Dialectic of enlightenment: Philosophical fragments.* Stanford University Press.

3. Bakker, E. (2009). *The Yearning for Zion: A study of a religious cult and its legal conflicts.* Journal of Religion and Law, 34(2), 128-145.

4. Benedict, R. (1935). *Patterns of culture.* Houghton Mifflin.

5. Boas, F. (1940). *Race, language, and culture.* Macmillan.

6. Bourdieu, P. (1973). *Cultural reproduction and social reproduction.* In R. Brown (Ed.), *Knowledge, education, and cultural change: Papers in the sociology of education* (pp. 71-112). Tavistock.

7. Geertz, C. (1973). *The interpretation of cultures: Selected essays.* Basic Books.

8. Geertz, C. (1973). *The interpretation of cultures: Selected essays.* Basic Books.

9. Giro, R. (2008). *Hipster: The history of an iconoclast.* Faber & Faber.

10. Good, B. (1993). *Medicine, rationality, and experience: An anthropological perspective.* Cambridge University Press.

11. Hebdige, D. (1979). *Subculture: The meaning of style.* Routledge.

12. Herskovits, M. J. (1958). *Cultural relativism: Perspectives in cultural pluralism.* Vintage Books.

13. Levi-Strauss, C. (1966). *The savage mind.* University of Chicago Press.

14. Levi-Strauss, C. (1970). *Mythologiques: Volume 1 - The raw and the cooked.* University of Chicago Press.

15. Levi-Strauss, C. (1973). *Mythologiques: Volume 2 - From honey to ashes.* University of Chicago Press.

16. Levi-Strauss, C. (1978). *Mythologiques: Volume 3 - The origin of table manners.* University of Chicago Press.

17. Levi-Strauss, C. (1981). *Mythologiques: Volume 4 - The intimacy of the outsiders.* University of Chicago Press.

18. Mauss, M. (1963). *The gift: The form and reason for exchange in archaic societies.* W.W. Norton & Company.

19. Murray, J. (2010). *Jazz and the rise of the hipster: The cultural legacy of the 1940s.* Journal of American Cultural Studies, 5(1), 23-45.

20. Nagel, T. (1986). *The view from nowhere.* Oxford University Press.

21. Radcliffe-Brown, A. R. (1952). *Structure and function in primitive society: Essays and addresses.* Free Press.

22. Sahlins, M. (1976). *Culture and practical reason.* University of Chicago Press.

23. Wittgenstein, L. (1953). *Philosophical investigations* (G. E. M. Anscombe, Trans.). Blackwell.

24. Zhang, X. (2020). *The development of China's cultural industry: A critique of Adorno's culture industry theory.* Journal of Chinese Culture Studies, 14(3), 78-92.

7. HORMONES - UNVEILING CLASSIFICATION

Shreeja, Ankitha G Bhat, Varsha B A and Mrs. Madhukala K L*

*Department of Lifesciences, Acharya Bangalore B School, Bengaluru, Karnataka, India
Email: madhukala.kl@abbs.edu.in

Abstract:

Body's biochemical messengers also called hormones, play a vital role in maintaining homeostasis, regulating physiological processes and facilitating unified communication between organs and tissues. These signaling molecules, secreted by endocrine glands, impact nearly every facet of animal biology, including growth, metabolism, reproduction, and behavior. In human biology, the earliest stages of embryonic development to the complexities of aging, hormones guide critical processes that ensure survival and adaptation to environmental changes. Their impact extends beyond individual systems, coordinating interactions between the nervous, immune, and endocrine systems to maintain equilibrium and respond to external stimuli. This chapter explores into the fascinating world of hormones, exploring their origins, intricate functions, and diverse mechanisms of action. A key focus is on the classification of hormones, which provides a understanding of their roles. Hormones can be categorized based on their origin, chemical composition—such as peptides, steroids, and amino acid derivatives—or their signaling pathways, including endocrine, paracrine, autocrine, and intracrine mechanisms. Functional classification further highlights their roles in processes like metabolism, growth, reproduction, and stress response. This comprehensive overview sheds light on how hormones interact with receptors and trigger cellular responses, emphasizing their precision and complexity. Understanding these classifications is essential not only for studying hormonal interactions but also for developing targeted therapies to address endocrine disorders and hormonal imbalances. By examining the origins, mechanisms, and diverse classifications of hormones, this chapter provides a robust foundation for appreciating their critical contributions to human physiology and health, offering insights into both normal biological processes and pathological conditions.

Keywords: Hormones, Endocrine, Autocrine, paracrine signaling, steroid, peptide, Ethylene.

1. Introduction:

For the body to function properly, its various organs must coordinate and communicate with each other to ensure that homeostasis is maintained. For example, the levels of salts, body temperature, etc., must be maintained in the body (Hiller-Sturmhöfel and Bartke, 1998). For communication and coordination in the body, two systems that play a major role are: the nervous system and the endocrine system. The nervous system rapidly transmits signals through cell-to-cell connections with the help of neurotransmitters. The endocrine system relies on endocrine glands that release chemical signals, called hormones, into blood that are transported to the specific tissues or organs. Major endocrine glands include the hypothalamus, the pituitary gland, pancreas, adrenal gland, thyroid and parathyroid (Leblebicioglu et al., 2013).

The word Hormone is derived from the Greek word "hormao" wich means "stimulate", "move" or "impulse" (Ioan, 2019). Hormones are organic substances formed in the endocrine glands, enter the blood stream, are transported via the blood stream to the target tissues or organs (Ahrorbek et al., 2023). Thus, hormones are chemical messengers that influence physical, physiological and behavioural changes (regulate metabolism, cell growth, division, differentiation, sleep cycle, mood changes, etc.,). Each hormone has target cells that are characterized by the presence of specific receptors either on the cell surface or inside the cell (Hiller-Sturmhöfel & Bartke, 1998). When the hormones are released, they initiate a series of reactions within the body, which finally result in the release of enzymes or changes in the cell (Emanuele et al., 1997).

2. Discovery of Hormone:

During the start of 20th century, an important discipline – Endocrinology was formulated that significantly improved our understanding of various regulatory processes (Starka and Duskova, 2020). In 1902, Ernest Henry Starling and William Maddock Bayliss identified secretin, a substance produced by the membrane of the duodenum. During the research, they discovered that the body's function was regulated by other factors, besides nerve impulses. Though they separated the nerves from the duodenum, the organ continued functioning. In 1904, Starling proposed that these substances should be called "hormones" (Ioan, 2019). Thus, the term "hormone" was first used by the physiologist Ernest Henry Starling in June, 1905 at the Croonian Lecture for the Royal College of Physicians (Starka and Duskova, 2020).

3. Classification of Hormones:

3.1. Based On Type of Organism:

> **Plant Hormone:** Plant hormones are a group of small molecules that help in plant growth and development (Nambara, 2017). They stimulate cell division, germination, root and fruit development (Abinash Chand Bharati, 2023). The plant hormones are grouped into

various classes like auxins, cytokinins, abscisic acid, gibberellins, ethylene, jasmonic acid, salicyclic acid, brassinosteroids and strigolactones based on their structural and chemical diversity (Chu, 2017).

➢ **Animal Hormone:** Hormones in animals are secreted by ductless glands called endocrine glands. These hormones help in growth, puberty, reproduction and metabolic processes like digestion, heart rate, respiration and psychological processes like emotions (Bharati, 2023).

3.2. Based On Cell Signaling (Cooper, 2000):

➢ **Endocrine Signaling:** In this type of signaling, the hormones are secreted by specialized endocrine cells and transport through blood to the target cells in the body. An example is estrogen, a female hormone produced in the ovaries, stimulates development and maintenance of female reproductive system and secondary sex characteristics.

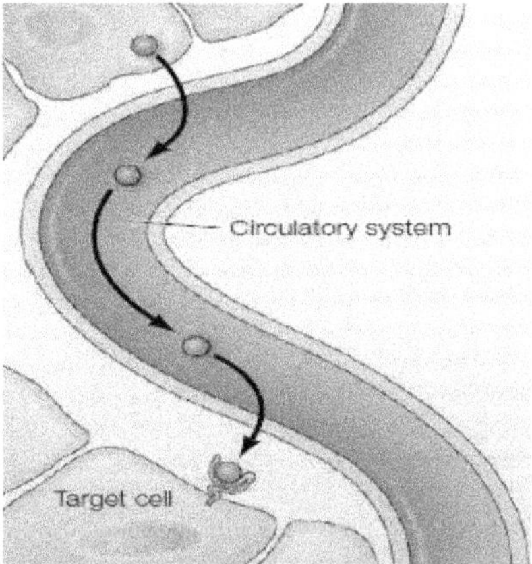

Figure 1: Endocrine Signaling

➢ **Paracrine Signaling:** In paracrine signalling, a molecule released by one cell induces changes in behaviour on neighbouring target cells. An example is provided by the action of neurotransmitters in carrying signals between nerve cells at a synapse.

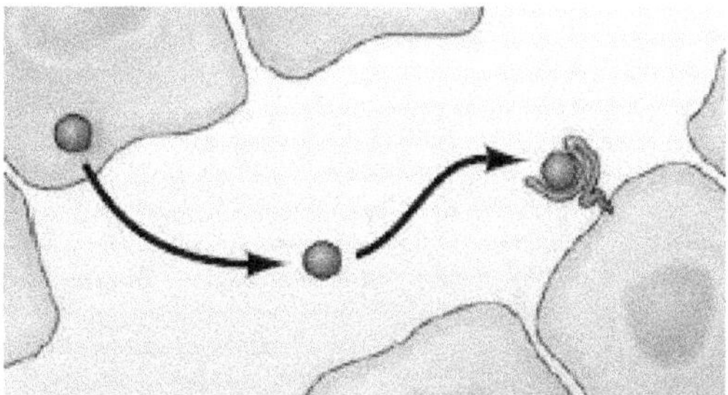

Figure 2: Paracrine Signaling

➢ **Autocrine Signaling:** Cell produces a chemical messenger that bind to the same cell's autocrine receptor. One important example of such autocrine signalling is the response of cells of the vertebrate immune system to foreign antigens. Certain types of T lymphocytes respond to antigenic stimulation by synthesising a growth factor that drives their own proliferation, thereby increasing the number of responsive T lymphocytes and amplifying the immune response.

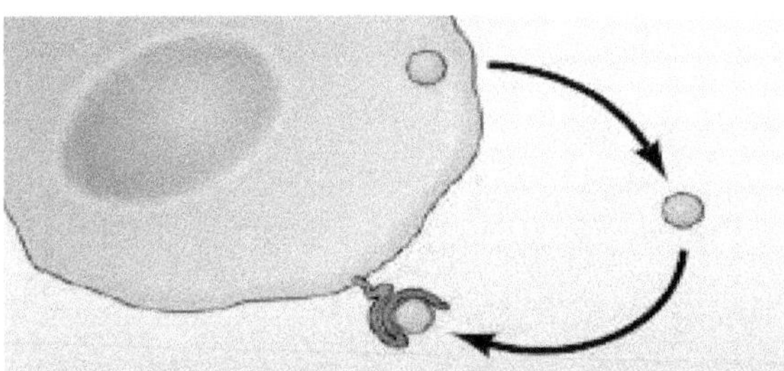

Figure 3: Autocrine Signaling

3.3. Based On Chemical Nature:

> **Peptide Hormone:** Peptide hormones are a class of signaling molecules composed of 10-100 amino acids that are secreted by endocrine glands. Once these hormones are released into the blood stream, they directly bind to the cell-receptor which triggers a various physiological change (Francesca Torrini, et al., 2023). Many polypeptide hormones are first synthesized as a larger inactive polypeptide. This inactive form is then cleaved by enzymes called endoproteases into a smaller active form (Mark Stamnes, 2004). Peptide hormones regulate a multitude of physiological diseases and changes in production or removal of these hormones and are associated with many diseases, including several types of tumours (Trier and Houen, 2017). For example, hormone insulin is converted to its active form by cleavage of the C-peptide. Some peptide hormones include: insulin, oxytocin, vasopressin, glucagon, etc.

> **Steroid Hormone:** Steroid hormones belong to a class of polycyclic and lipophilic chemicals that have major physiological effects on the body (Lagrange and Kelly, 2003). These hormones are derived form a precursor molecule called cholesterol (Andersson, 2008). Steroid hormones are extremely active biological compounds which produce intensive effects at low doses. Four classes of steroid hormones include oestrogens, androgens, progestogens, and glucocorticoids (Ying, 2013). Steroids have an important role in growth, development, sexual differentiation and reproduction Adhya, et al., 2018).

- ➤ **Amino Acid Derivative Hormones**: The amino acid derived hormones are relatively small hydrophobic molecules which are derived from tyrosine and tryptophan amino acids. They play a major role in the regulation of organism development and other metabolic processes (Jiang, 2023). One example is Carnitine is an amino acid derived hormone synthesized by lysine and methionine which plays a vital role in oxidation of fatty acids (Wang, 2022). Other examples include D-penicillamine, histidine, lysine, leucine, etc.

- ➤ **Gaseous Molecules as Hormones**: Ethylene is the only gaseous plant hormone. it is helpful in fruit ripening, seedling growth, root hair formation (Sisler and Yang, 1984). Nitrous oxide, a simple gas, acts as a major paracrine signaling molecule in the nervous, immune and circulatory systems. NO can directly diffuse through the plasma membrane of its target cells (Cooper. 2000).

3.4. Based On Effect (Choudhary, 2024):

- ➤ **Metabolic Hormone:** This hormone functions to regulate the rate of metabolism and balance the reaction in the body. Examples – glucagon, PTH, insulin, etc.
- ➤ **Morphogenic Hormone:** The hormones responsible for growth and differentiation play a role in these processes. Examples – FSH, STH, thyroid hormones, LTH, etc.

3.5. Based On Mechanism of Action:

- ➤ **Lipophilic Hormone:** These are hydrophobic or fat-soluble hormones. They can easily pass through cell membranes as they are lipid soluble. Some of the hormones are steroid hormones like testosterone etc
- ➤ **Lipophobic Hormone:** These are hydrophilic or water-soluble hormones. They can't pass through cell membranes; hence they are transported through transport proteins. Some of them include amines, peptides, glycoproteins etc.

4. Mechanism of Action of Hormone:

4.1. Water-Soluble Hormone (Catt and Dufau, 1976):

- Water-soluble hormone combines with their specific receptor sites in the plasma membrane of their target cells. This is followed by rapid activation of cellular responses.
- These responses are initiated by the action of cyclic AMP (cAMP), formed by adenylate cyclase which is activated by the hormone-receptor interaction.
- This cAMP acts as a secondary messenger which then activates protein kinase enzyme.

- Protein kinase causes phosphorylation of specific substrate which regulate target cell functions.

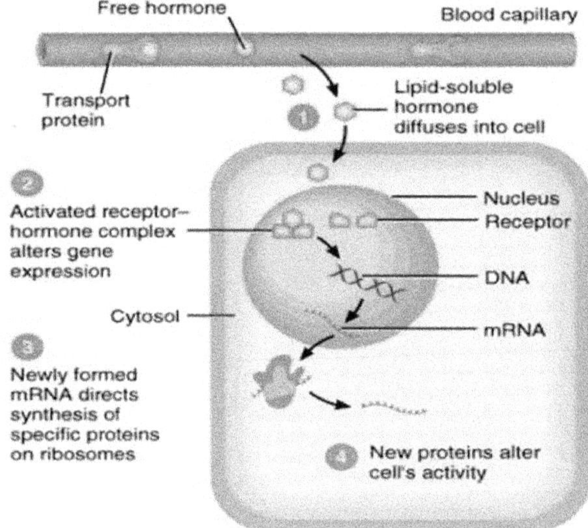

Figure 4: Mechanism of Action of Lipid-Soluble Hormone

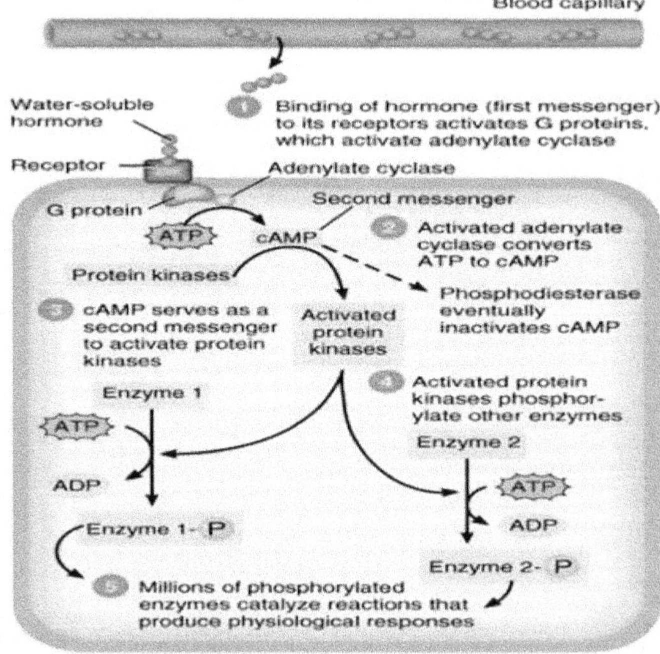

Figure 5: Mechanism of Action of water-Soluble Hormone

4.1. Fat-Soluble Hormone (Edelman, 1976):

- The hormone diffuses through the cell membrane into the target cell.
- The hormone stereo-specifically binds to the high affinity receptors.
- Temperature sensitive activation of hormone-receptor complex.
- The active complex induces transcription of RNA followed by protein synthesis.
- The synthesized protein alters the functions of the cell.

5. Hormones And Their Effects:

5.1. Testosterone: Testosterone is the major male hormone produced in testes by relaying signals from pituitary gland and a small amount is produced by adrenal glands. This hormone functions in regulating variations in sex characteristics, gametogenesis in males, fertility and production of male secondary characteristics (Nassar and Leslie, 2023). It is mainly secreted in males and by ovaries in females (to less extent). Greater production of testosterone occurs in males (4-12 mg per day) than in females (Usmani and Kant, 2021). At first, the fetus experiences the effects of testosterone. The reproductive tissues of males and females are similar during initial 6 weeks of fetal development. Around 7th week of pregnancy, the Y

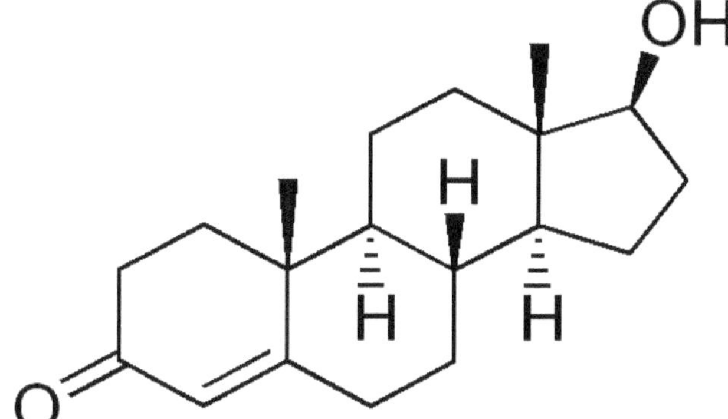

Figure 6: **Structure:** Testosterone (Usmani and Kant, 2021).

chromosome (SRY) drives the development of the testicles. Seminiferous tubules are produced from Sertoli cells in the testis cords. The Mullerian-inhibiting substance (MIS) produced by Sertoli cells will regress fallopian tubes, uterus and upper part of vaginal canal (Nassar and Leslie, 2023). It has major influence on body fat composition and muscle mass in the male (Kelly and Jones, 2013). It helps to maintain hair growth and muscle strength and also developing tissues like testis, prostate, seminal vesicles, epididymis (Usmani and Kant, 2021). It is a steroid hormone which is derived from cholesterol. It leads to higher hematocrit in males which is erythropoiesis. This hormone tends to decrease with age (Nassar and Leslie, 2023).

EFFECTS (Usmani and Kant, 2021).

- Testosterone results in increased libido.
- Development of muscle and bone strength.
- It stimulates hematopoiesis by increasing the production of erythropoietin.
- Low level of testosterone enhances high risk of cardiovascular disease.
- Subcutaneous fat in face decreases.
- Deepening of voice.
- Inflating bone reabsorption.

- Diabetes mellitus is caused because of reduced testosterone.
- Helps in growth of excessive hair on face and armpits.

5.2. Glucagon: Glucagon consisting of 29 amino acids is a straight chain polypeptide hormone. It is secreted by alpha cells of the Islets of Langerhans (Kaneko, 2008). Molecular weight of glucagon is 3485 Da. Being a member of PACAP family of peptides, it is relatable to secretin and CCK (Norris and Carr, 2013). Hypoglycemia stimulates the release of glucagon (Kaneko, 2008). Glucagon promotes gluconeogenesis and glycogenolysis by increasing the blood glucose levels. It plays an important role in the liver and also affects adipose tissue, pancreas, brain and kidney (Tachibana, 2021). This is necessary for regulation of carbohydrate and lipid in vertebrates. It plays an important role in counter-regulatory activities with insulin in the control of blood metabolites (Moon, 1998). Initially it functions by binding to the surface receptors on the cell (Kaneko, 2008). It also acts as insulin releasing which is basis for glucagon stimulation test (GST). It helps lipolysis in the adipose tissues and in releasing glucose from the liver's glycogen reservoirs (Sirhan and Piran, 2022). It acts as rescue for hypoglycemic events (Lima and Icart, 2022). When circulating glucose is low in human system, results in release of glucagon into bloodstream which in turn stimulates output of hepatic glucose leading to increase in glycemia thereby providing a counter regulatory mechanism to insulin in maintaining glucose homeostasis in vivo. (Jiang and Zhang, 2003). Glucagon increases energy expenditure (Habeggar et al., 2010). By stimulation of glycogen breakdown and activation of gluconeogenesis within the liver results in increase of blood glucose level concentration (Dotson and Munger, 2013). It stimulates mobilization of fats and breakdown of triglyceride (Cole and Eastoe, 1988).

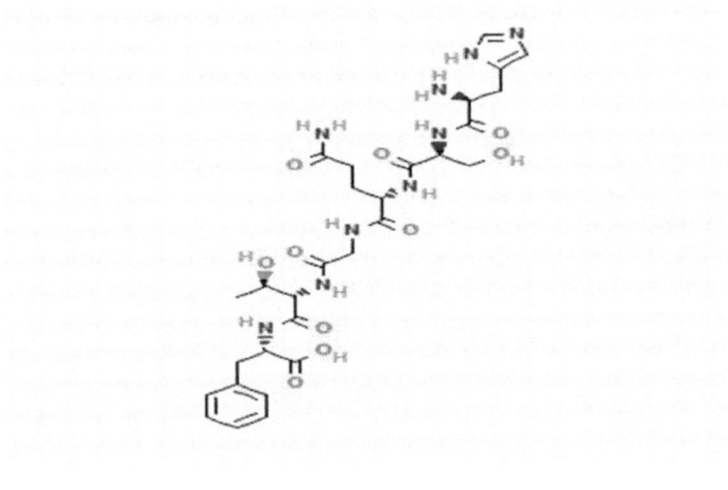

Figure 7: **Structure:** Glucagon (National Centre for Biotechnology Information-2024)

EFFECTS (Rix et al., 2019)

- Glucagon stimulates hepatic conversion of glycogen to glucose.
- It contributes to a stable energy homeostasis during increased energy demand.
- It results in formation of glucose from amino acids.
- Glucagon activates brown adipose tissue.
- It increases heart rate.
- It helps in cardiac contractility.
- Promotes formation of non-carbohydrate energy sources such as lipid and ketone bodies.
- It stimulates ketogenesis.

5.3. Estrogen: Estrogen is the major steroid hormone synthesized from ovaries which plays a vital role in female reproduction as it controls menstrual cycle (Hamilton et al.,2017). Estrone, estradiol estriol are the forms of estrogen of which estradiol is very common for hormone replacement therapy in treating the symptoms of menopause (Delgado and Lopez-Ojeda, 2023). Estrogen works through its 2 distinct nuclear receptors, estrogen receptors, estrogen receptor alpha and estrogen receptor beta (Hamilton et al., 2017). Estrogen influences on obesity, osteoporosis, cancer, endometriosis and fibroids (Derro and Korach, 2006). Estrogen action takes place through nuclear estrogen receptor expression in estrogen target organs. (Mangelsdorf et al., 1995).

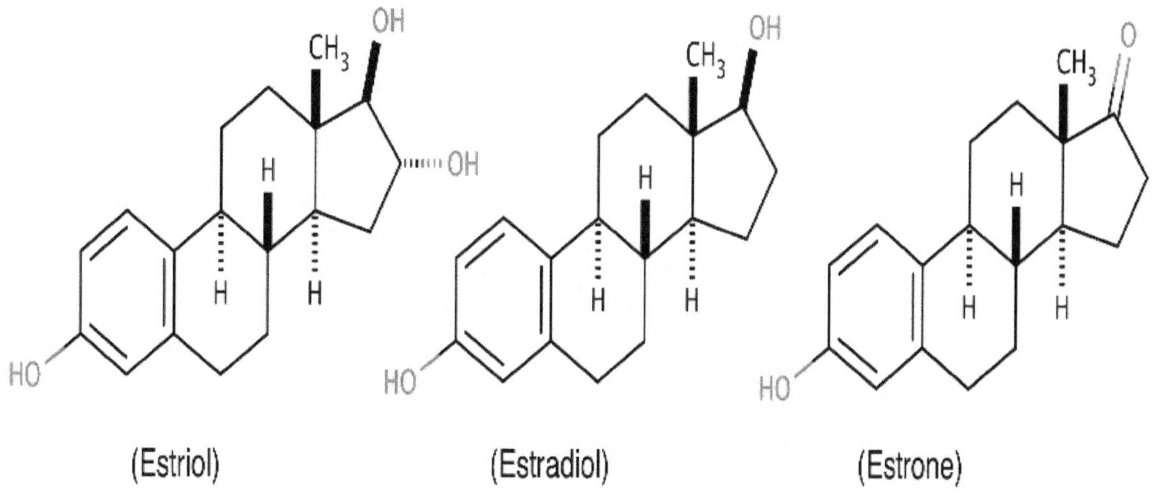

Figure 8: Structure: Estrogen (Benjamin J Delgado and Wilfredo Lopez-Ojeda, 2023).

EFFECTS (Delgado and Lopez-Ojeda, 2023).

- Estrogen is crucial for development of mammary gland tissue and ducts.
- It supports proliferation of epithelial mucosa cells of vagina.
- It helps in thickening of endometrial lining.
- It functions to secrete milk in postpartum lactation.
- Estrogen aids fusion of the epiphyseal growth plates.
- It protects bones thereby preventing osteoporosis.

5.4. Epinephrine: Epinephrine or adrenaline is a 'fight or flight hormone produced and stored in the chromaffin cells of the adrenal medulla releasing when signaling of SNS occurs with resultant physiological effects (Skelding and Valverde, 2020). It makes potent vasopressor as it is a strong alpha and beta-adrenergic agonist (Hurcombe, 2018). Alpha receptors respond better to norepinephrine and epinephrine are responded by beta receptors (Feher, 2012). Epinephrine is usually fast but short lived. Adrenaline which is a neurotransmitter is released from adrenal glands into the bloodstream during stress or anger (Al-Shura, 2021). Based on receptor expression of tissue action of epinephrine takes place like this hormone contracts the smooth muscles that are lining arterioles and relaxes which are lining esophagus. It is also a non-selective agonist of all adrenergic receptors (Azmitia, 2012). In humans there is slight decrease in basal plasma EPI concentrations with respect to increasing age. (Lupien and Fiocco, 2009).

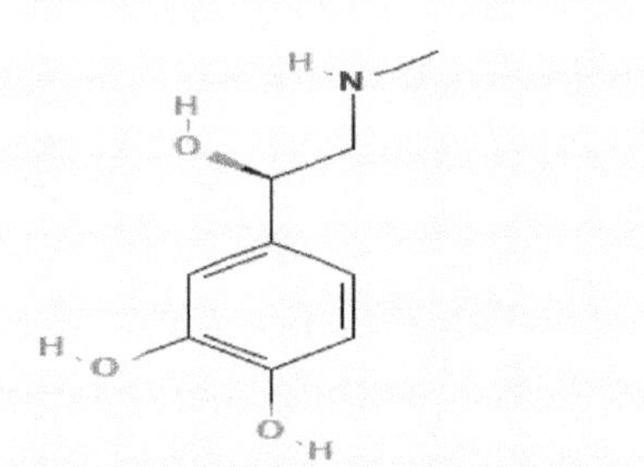

Figure 9: Structure: Epinephrine (National Center for Biotechnology Information -2024)

EFFECTS (Dalal and Grujic, 2023; Papich, 2016)

- It is primarily used to treat cardiopulmonary arrest and anaphylactic shock.
- It leads to increase in heart rate.
- It causes contraction in blood vessels.
- It leads to vomiting, nausea and headaches.

5.5. Cortisol: Cortisol is the major glucocorticoid released from the zona fasciculata layer of the adrenal cortex (Mendelson, 2008). During times of circadian rhythm, it is released in small amounts and in layer amounts during physiologic stress (Burkitt, 2009). Both production and secretion of cortisol is regulated by hypothalamus - pituitary - adrenal axis (Thau et al., 2023). For clinical use it is measured in serum, urine and saliva (Vega-Beyhart et al., 2023). It plays a virtual role in maintaining serum glucose levels in the body (Mendelson, 2008). It also operates like mineralocorticoid which is produced by inter-renal tissue under the control of adrenocorticotropic hormone (Mommesen et al., 1999). Cortisol is shown to rise anywhere from 2 to 4-fold in maternal serum over the cause of gestation (Davis and Sandman, 2010). It has capacity to block the ability of insulin to increase the uptake of glucose into adipose and muscle cells (Mendelson, 2008). Cortisol is critical in diagnosis of Cushing's syndrome and Addison's disease (Nieman, 2003).

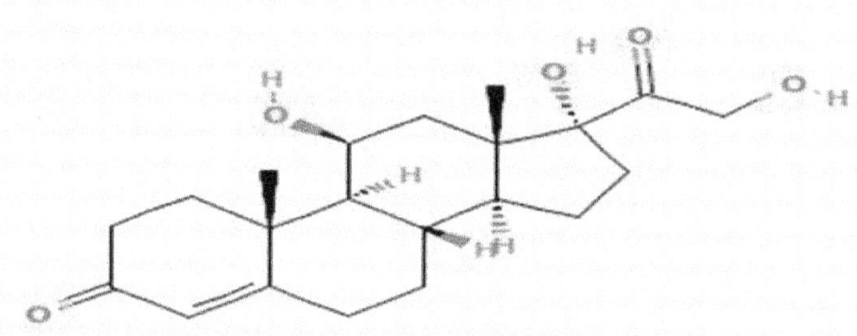

Figure 10: Structure: Cortisol (National Center for Biotechnology Information -2024)

EFFECTS (Ashton, 2023)

- Cortisol supresses the immune system.
- It increases blood sugar.
- Increases the blood pressure.

6. Conclusion:

Understanding hormones in facet with their systematic approach to classification not only enriches our knowledge of human physiology but also lays the foundation for significant advancements in medical science. It is especially vital for improving the diagnosis and treatment of hormone-related disorders, which can overpoweringly impact overall health and well-being. However, further it is essential to fully unstitch the intricate mechanisms and interactions of hormonal systems, including the complex changing aspects of hormonal axes and their influence on human development and health.

References:

1. Adhya, D., Annuario, E., Lancaster, M. A., Price, J., Baron-Cohen, S., & Srivastava, D. P. (2018). Understanding the role of steroids in typical and atypical brain development: Advantages of using a "brain in a dish" approach. *Journal of Neuroendocrinology, 30*(2), e12547. https://doi.org/10.1111/jne.12547

2. Andersson, H. (2008). Clinical reproductive endocrinology. In *Clinical biochemistry of domestic animals* (6th ed., pp. 635-662). Academic Press. https://doi.org/10.1016/B978-0-12-370491-7.00021-0

3. Al-Shura, A. N. (2021). Humoral control. In *Mechanisms of action in disease and recovery in integrative cardiovascular Chinese medicine* (pp. 59-62). Academic Press. https://doi.org/10.1016/B978-0-12-817578-1.00008-2

4. Ashton, C. M. (2023). Biological bases of personality. In *Individual differences and personality* (4th ed., pp. 111-129). Academic Press. https://doi.org/10.1016/B978-0-323-85950-9.00007-8

5. Azmitia, E. C. (2012). Brain chemicals: Global projections of ancient aromatic neurotransmitters. In *Encyclopaedia of human behaviour* (2nd ed., pp. 396-405). Academic Press. https://doi.org/10.1016/B978-0-12-375000-6.00069-0

6. Bharati, C. A., Prasad, B., Mallick, S., Masram, S. D., Kumar, A., & Saxena, K. G. (2023). Animal and plant hormones. In *Handbook of biomolecules* (pp. 151-175). https://doi.org/10.1016/B978-0-323-91684-4.00028-1

7. Burkitt, M. J. (2009). Relative adrenal insufficiency. In *Small animal critical care medicine* (pp. 318-320). https://doi.org/10.1016/B978-1-4160-2591-7.10075-X

8. Butnariu, M., & Ioan, S. (2019). Biochemistry of hormones that influence feelings. *Pharmacoepidemiology and Drug Safety, 1,* 1-6. https://www.researchgate.net/publication/334561821

9. Catt, J. K., & Dufau, L. M. (1976). Basic concepts of the mechanism of action of peptide hormones. *Biology of Reproduction, 14*(1), 1-15. https://doi.org/10.1095/biolreprod14.1.1

10. Choudary, A. (2024). Classification of hormones, mechanism of hormone action. *Pharmaguideline.*

11. Chu, J., Fang, S., Xin, P., Guo, Z., & Chen, Y. (2017). Quantitative analysis of plant hormones based on LC-MS/MS. In *Hormone metabolism and signaling in plants* (pp. 471-537). Academic Press. https://doi.org/10.1016/B978-0-12-811562-6.00014-1

12. Cole, A. S., & Eastoe, J. E. (1988). Hormones and growth factors. In *Biochemistry and oral biology* (pp. 345-367). Butterworth-Heinemann. https://doi.org/10.1016/B978-0-7236-1751-8.50031-4

13. Cooper, G. M. (2000). *The cell: A molecular approach* (2nd ed.). Sinauer Associates.

14. Davis, E. P., & Sandman, C. A. (2010). The timing of prenatal exposure to maternal cortisol and psychosocial stress is associated with human infant cognitive development. *Child Development, 81*(1), 131–148. https://doi.org/10.1111/j.1467-8624.2009.01385.x

15. Dalal, R., & Grujic, D. (2023). Epinephrine. In *StatPearls* (Treasure Island, FL: StatPearls Publishing). Available from: https://www.ncbi.nlm.nih.gov/books/NBK482160/

16. De Kloet, E. R. (2004). Hormones and the stressed brain. *Annals of the New York Academy of Sciences, 1018*, 1–15. https://doi.org/10.1196/annals.1296.001

17. Delgado, B. J., & Lopez-Ojeda, W. (2023). Estrogen. In *StatPearls* (Treasure Island, FL: StatPearls Publishing). Available from: https://www.ncbi.nlm.nih.gov/books/NBK538260/

18. Deroo, B. J., & Korach, K. S. (2006). Estrogen receptors and human disease. *The Journal of Clinical Investigation, 116*(3), 561–570. https://doi.org/10.1172/JCI27987

19. Dotson, C. D., Geraedts, M. C., & Munger, S. D. (2013). Peptide regulators of peripheral taste function. *Seminars in Cell & Developmental Biology, 24*(3), 232–239. https://doi.org/10.1016/j.semcdb.2013.01.004

20. Edelman, I. S. (1976). Mechanism of action of steroid hormones. In *Proceedings of the fourth international congress on hormonal steroids* (pp. 147-159). https://doi.org/10.1016/B978-0-08-019682-4.50006-8

21. Emanuele, N., & Emanuele, M. A. (1997). The endocrine system: Alcohol alters critical hormonal balance. Alcohol Health and Research World, 21(1), 53–64.

22. Feher, J. (2012). Regulation of perfusion. In Quantitative human physiology (2nd ed., pp. 589–598). Academic Press. https://doi.org/10.1016/B978-0-12-800883-6.00056-2

23. Habegger, K. M., Heppner, K. M., Geary, N., Bartness, T. J., DiMarchi, R., & Tschöp, M. H. (2010). The metabolic actions of glucagon revisited. Nature Reviews Endocrinology, 6(12), 689–697. https://doi.org/10.1038/nrendo.2010.187

24. Hackney, A. C., & Lane, A. R. (2015). Exercise and the regulation of endocrine hormones. Progress in Molecular Biology and Translational Science, 135, 293–311. https://doi.org/10.1016/bs.pmbts.2015.07.001

25. Hamilton, K. J., Hewitt, S. C., Arao, Y., & Korach, K. S. (2017). Estrogen hormone biology. In Current Topics in Developmental Biology (Vol. 125, pp. 109–146). Academic Press. https://doi.org/10.1016/bs.ctdb.2016.12.005

26. Hiller-Sturmhöfel, S., & Bartke, A. (1998). The endocrine system: An overview. Alcohol Health and Research World, 22(3), 153–164.

27. Hurcombe, D. S. (2018). Chapter 4- Critical care. In Equine Internal Medicine (4th ed., pp. 158–190). https://doi.org/10.1016/B978-0-323-44329-6.00004-8

28. Jiang, G., & Zhang, B. B. (2003). Glucagon and regulation of glucose metabolism. American Journal of Physiology. Endocrinology and Metabolism, 284(4), E671–E678. https://doi.org/10.1152/ajpendo.00492.2002

29. Jiang, J., Li, J., Gao, Y., Li, M., & Long, Y. (2023). Direct identification of amino acid derived hormones with single atom resolution using an engineered aerolysin nanopore. Biophysical Journal, 122(3), 288a. https://doi.org/10.1016/j.bpj.2022.11.1635

30. Kaneko, J. J. (2008). Clinical biochemistry of domestic animals. Carbohydrate metabolism and its diseases. In Clinical Biochemistry of Domestic Animals (6th ed., pp. 45–80). Academic Press. https://doi.org/10.1016/B978-0-12-370491-7.00003-9

31. Kelly, D. M., & Jones, T. H. (2013). Testosterone: A metabolic hormone in health and disease. Journal of Endocrinology, 217(3), R25–R45. https://doi.org/10.1530/JOE-12-0455

32. Lagrange, H. A., & Kelly, J. M. (2003). Neuroactive steroids. In Encyclopaedia of Hormones (pp. 8–19). Academic Press. https://doi.org/10.1016/B0-12-341103-3/00212-6

33. Leblebicioglu, B., Connors, J., & Mariotti, A. (2013). Principles of endocrinology. Periodontology 2000, 61(1), 54–68. https://doi.org/10.1111/j.1600-0757.2011.00440.x

34. Lima, L. M. T. R., & Icart, L. P. (2022). Amyloidogenicity of peptides targeting diabetes and obesity. Colloids and Surfaces B: Biointerfaces, 209, 112157. https://doi.org/10.1016/j.colsurfb.2021.112157

35. Lupien, S. J., Lord, C., Sindi, S., Wilkinson, C. W., & Fiocco, A. J. (2009). Aging and Alzheimer's disease. In Hormones, Brain and Behaviour (Vol. 2, pp. 3049–3083). Academic Press. https://doi.org/10.1016/B978-008088783-8.00097-8

36. Mangelsdorf, D. J., Thummel, C., Beato, M., Herrlich, P., Schütz, G., Umesono, K., Blumberg, B., Kastner, P., Mark, M., Chambon, P., & Evans, R. M. (1995). The nuclear

receptor superfamily: The second decade. Cell, 83(6), 835–839. https://doi.org/10.1016/0092-8674(95)90199-x

37. Mendelson, S. D. (2008). Metabolic syndrome and psychiatric illness: The pathophysiology of metabolic syndrome. In Metabolic Syndrome (pp. 27–48). https://doi.org/10.1016/b978-012374240-7.50005-x

38. Mommsen, T. P., Vijayan, M. M., & Moon, T. W. (1999). Cortisol in teleosts: Dynamics, mechanisms of action, and metabolic regulation. Reviews in Fish Biology and Fisheries, 9, 211–268. https://doi.org/10.1023/A:1008924418720

39. Moon, W. T. (1998). Glucagon: From hepatic binding to metabolism in teleost fish. Comparative Biochemistry and Physiology Part B: Biochemistry and Molecular Biology, 121(1), 27–34. https://doi.org/10.1016/S0305-0491(98)10108-6

40. Nambara, E. (2017). Plant hormone. In Reference Module in Life Science. https://doi.org/10.1016/B978-0-12-809633-8.06912-0

41. Nieman, L. K., Biller, B. M., Findling, J. W., Newell-Price, J., Savage, M. O., Stewart, P. M., & Montori, V. M. (2008). The diagnosis of Cushing's syndrome: An Endocrine Society Clinical Practice Guideline. The Journal of Clinical Endocrinology and Metabolism, 93(5), 1526–1540. https://doi.org/10.1210/jc.2008-0125

42. Nuraliev, A., Ahrorbek, L., Lee, M., Lee, J., Jae, H., Lee, S., & Salimova, D. E. (2023). Hormonal regulation. Texas Journal of Multidisciplinary Studies, 25, 39–43. Retrieved from https://zienjournals.com/index.php/tjm/article/view/4476

43. Nassar, G. N., & Leslie, S. W. (2023). Physiology, testosterone. In StatPearls. Treasure Island (FL): StatPearls Publishing. Available from https://www.ncbi.nlm.nih.gov/books/NBK526128/

44. Norris, D. O., & Carr, J. A. (2013). Chemical regulation of feeding, digestion, and metabolism. In Vertebrate endocrinology (pp. 443–481). https://doi.org/10.1016/b978-0-12-394815-1.00012-4

45. Papich, G. M. (2016). Epinephrine. In Saunders handbook of veterinary drugs (4th ed., pp. 291–292). W. B. Saunders. https://doi.org/10.1016/B978-0-323-24485-5.00242-4

46. Sirhan, W., & Piran, R. (2022). Therapeutic peptidomimetics in metabolic diseases. In Advances in clinical chemistry (pp. 521–550). Academic Press. https://doi.org/10.1016/B978-0-12-820141-1.00023-6

47. Sisler, C. E., & Yang, F. S. (1984). The gaseous plant hormone. Bioscience, 34(4), 234–238. https://doi.org/10.2307/1309461

48. Skelding, M. A., & Valverde, A. (2020). Sympathomimetics in veterinary species under anaesthesia. The Veterinary Journal, 258, 105455. https://doi.org/10.1016/j.tvjl.2020.105455

49. Stamnes, M. (2004). Golgi complex. In Encyclopaedia of biological chemistry (pp. 312–315). Elsevier. https://doi.org/10.1016/B0-12-443710-9/00286-6

50. Starka, L., & Duskova, M. (2020). What is a hormone? Physiological Research, 69, S183–S185. Czech Academy of Sciences. https://doi.org/10.33549/physiolres.934509

51. Tachibana, T. (2021). Glucagon. In Handbook of hormones (2nd ed., pp. 231–234). Academic Press. https://doi.org/10.1016/B978-0-12-820649-2.00061-9

52. Thau, L., Gandhi, J., & Sharma, S. (2023). Physiology, cortisol. In StatPearls. Treasure Island (FL): StatPearls Publishing. Available from https://www.ncbi.nlm.nih.gov/books/NBK538239/

53. Torrini, F., Scarano, S., Palladino, P., & Minunni, M. (2023). Advances and perspectives in the analytical technology for small peptide hormones analysis: A glimpse of gonadorelin. Journal of Pharmaceutical and Biomedical Analysis, 228, 115312. https://doi.org/10.1016/j.jpba.2023.115312

54. Trier, H. N., & Houen, G. (2017). Peptide antibodies in clinical laboratory diagnostics. In Advances in clinical chemistry (Vol. 81, pp. 43–96). https://doi.org/10.1016/bs.acc.2017.01.002

55. Usmani, H., & Kant, R. (2021). Testosterone: An insight into its clinical and biochemical assessments. Indian Journal of Medical Biochemistry, 25(1), 24–30. https://doi.org/10.5005/jp-journals-10054-0173

56. Vega-Beyhart, A., Araujo-Castro, M., Hanzu, A. F., & Casals, G. (2023). Cortisol: Analytical and clinical determinants. In Advances in Clinical Chemistry (Vol. 113, pp. 235–271). Elsevier. https://doi.org/10.1016/bs.acc.2022.11.005

57. Wang, Y. A. (2022). Nutrition and anaemia in chronic kidney disease. In Nutritional management of renal disease (pp. 741–760). Academic Press. https://doi.org/10.1016/B978-0-12-818540-7.00035-5

58. Ying, G., Zhao, J., Zhou, L., & Liu, S. (2013). Fate and occurrence of pharmaceuticals in the aquatic environment (surface water and sediment). In Comprehensive analytical chemistry (Vol. 62, pp. 453–557). https://doi.org/10.1016/B978-0-444-62657-8.00014-8

8. EVOLUTION, NATURAL SELECTION AND PRACTICAL EXAMPLES

N. Sai Prashanthi

Department of microbiology, Osmania university, Hyderabad

Email: saiprashanthi.neelda@gmail.com

Abstract:

Evolution, the process through which species undergo transformations over time, is fundamentally driven by natural selection—a mechanism that promotes the prevalence of traits enhancing an organism's survival and reproductive success across generations. Natural selection occurs when variations in traits are present within a population, some of which provide advantageous characteristics in a specific environment. Over time, these beneficial traits become increasingly common, resulting in evolutionary change. This process is crucial for the emergence of new species and their adaptation to fluctuating environments. Practical examples of natural selection manifest in both natural and controlled settings. One notable instance is the evolution of the peppered moth in England, where moth populations altered their coloration in response to industrial pollution. Another significant example is antibiotic resistance in bacteria, which has emerged because of the excessive use of antibiotics, leading to the survival of resistant strains. These instances illustrate how natural selection influences the genetic composition of populations, highlighting its critical role in deciphering biological diversity and adaptation. However, understanding these mechanisms requires a nuanced approach, as the interplay of various factors can complicate straightforward interpretations.
Key words: evolution, natural selection, life, adaptations, traits.

1. Introduction:

Evolution means simply change over time; organic evolution refers to descent with modification over time. It explains how life originated and evolved on Earth. Evolution represents the mechanism through which various species of organisms undergo transformation over time, primarily as a result of alterations in their genetic composition (Futuyma & Kirkpatrick, 2017). This process elucidates the remarkable diversity of life on Earth, revealing how organisms adapt to distinct environments and ecological niches. Evolution occurs across generations, propelled by the gradual accumulation of minor genetic changes, which can ultimately result in the emergence of new species (Mayr, 2001).

Natural selection, a fundamental aspect of evolution, was introduced by Charles Darwin in the 19th century. It is the mechanism by which specific traits gain prevalence within a population because they enhance the likelihood of survival and reproduction among individuals who exhibit those traits (Darwin, 1859). Over time, these beneficial characteristics are transmitted to subsequent generations, thereby instigating evolutionary shifts within the population. However, the complexity of these processes cannot be understated, as multiple factors can influence the trajectory of evolutionary change (Dobzhansky, 1973).

Key Principles of Natural Selection:

Variation: Within any specific population, individuals exhibit variations in their characteristics (for instance, size, color, behavior). Inheritance: These characteristics are passed down from parents to their offspring through genetic material. Differential Survival and Reproduction: Individuals possessing traits that are more suited to their environment tend to survive and reproduce at higher rates, thus allowing them to pass on those traits. Adaptation: Over time, the population as a whole may become increasingly well adapted to its environment, however, this occurs because advantageous traits tend to proliferate (Hendry et al., 2011).

2. The Theory of Evolution:

Charles Darwin's seminal work, On the Origin of Species (1859), greatly advanced the discourse on natural selection. His observations during the voyage aboard the HMS Beagle—particularly in the Galápagos Islands—led him to postulate that species undergo evolution over time through incremental changes. He noted that species inhabiting distinct islands shared ancestral lineages; however, they exhibited unique characteristics tailored to their specific environments. Evolution occurs through several key mechanisms: genetic variation (where mutations and genetic recombination promote diversity within populations), inheritance (where advantageous traits for survival are passed on to progeny), overproduction of offspring (because organisms often produce more offspring than their environments can sustain, leading to competition for limited resources) and differential survival and reproduction (where individuals endowed with traits better suited to their surroundings have a higher likelihood of surviving and reproducing, thus ensuring the continuation of these advantageous traits into future generations (Smith, 1958).

Although the mechanisms of evolution are intricate, this framework offers a thorough understanding of how species adapt over time. Although these mechanisms elucidate the process of evolution, the complexities inherent to ecological interactions render the concept of evolution multifaceted. This complexity stems from numerous factors, including environmental changes and species interactions. However, grasping these dynamics is crucial, because they significantly influence evolutionary trajectories. Evolution is not a simple process; it is shaped by various elements that intertwine and engage with each other (MacConaill and Stebbins 1972).

3. Evidence for Evolution:

An abundance of evidentiary lines underpins the evolutionary paradigm: the fossil record offers a chronological sequence of life forms (documenting the transformation of species over time). Transitional fossils—such as Archaeopteryx (which serves as a critical link between dinosaurs and avian species)—provide further support for evolutionary mechanisms. Comparative anatomy demonstrates that an analysis of homologous structures (body parts exhibiting similarity across diverse species due to shared ancestry) reinforces the idea of common descent. For instance, the forelimbs of humans, whales and bats display analogous bone structures; however, they fulfill different functions. This indicates a shared lineage. In the realm of molecular biology, the emergence of DNA sequencing has revealed a vast amount of evidence bolstering evolutionary theory. Genetic similarities among species, including humans and chimpanzees, highlight an ancestral relationship. The greater the genetic similarity, the more closely related the species tend to be Sober, 2008))

3.1. Comparative Anatomy: The examination of homologous structures (i.e., anatomical features exhibiting similarities across various species due to a shared ancestry) bolsters the concept of common descent. For instance, the forelimbs of humans, whales and bats, although employed for distinct functions, exhibit similar bone structures. This resemblance indicates a common ancestor (Gibbins, 2021).

3.2. Molecular Biology: DNA sequencing has yielded an abundance of evidence supporting the theory of evolution. The genetic similarities noted between species—such as humans and chimpanzees—underscore the notion of shared ancestry. However, the greater the genetic similarity, the more closely related the species are likely to be(Osawa et al., 1991).

3.3. Embryology: The preliminary developmental phases of various vertebrates (for example, humans, chickens and fish) demonstrate striking similarities, indicating a shared evolutionary lineage. Evolution, propelled by natural selection, acts as a fundamental engine that promotes (1) the diversity and adaptation of life on Earth. The theory, initially proposed by Darwin, has received considerable backing from fields such as paleontology, genetics and comparative anatomy; however, real-world examples (e.g., the evolution of the peppered moth, Darwin's finches and antibiotic resistance in bacteria) exemplify how natural selection shapes the characteristics of species over time. Understanding these mechanisms is essential for disciplines ranging from conservation biology to medicine, because it provides crucial insights into how organisms interact with their environments and how species adjust to ecological changes. Although this understanding remains important, it is often disregarded in light of more urgent matters (Osawa et al., 1991).

4. Natural Selection: Mechanism and Process:

Natural selection operates through the variations that exist within a given population (Kolman, 1960). It is underpinned by four fundamental principles:

4.1. Variation: Individuals within a population exhibit a range of traits—such as color, size, or shape. These variations may emerge because of mutations or genetic recombination.

4.2. Competition: Resources—like food, space and mates—are finite; therefore, organisms must compete for survival and reproduction.

4.3. Survival of the Fittest: Organisms that possess advantageous traits tend to be more likely to survive and reproduce, thus passing these traits onto their offspring. The notion of "fitness" pertains to an organism's capacity to thrive and reproduce in a specific environment.

4.4. Adaptation: Over many generations, natural selection can result in the accumulation of beneficial traits within a population, leading to the adaptation of species to their distinct environments. However, this process is not immediate; it necessitates substantial time and environmental pressures to influence the evolutionary trajectory of a species

Evolutionary processes lead to adaptation, wherein species gradually become more suited to their environments over time— Evolution occurs through several crucial mechanisms:

- ➢ **Genetic Variation:** (Mutations and genetic recombination create diversity within populations).
- ➢ **Inheritance:** (Traits advantageous for survival are passed down to offspring).
- ➢ **Overproduction of Offspring:** (organisms typically produce more offspring than the environment can support, resulting in competition for resources).

> ➤ **Differential Survival and Reproduction:** (Individuals with traits better suited to their environment are more likely to survive and reproduce, thus passing these traits to future generations.

5. Four Practical Examples of Natural Selection:

One notable case is the peppered moth (Biston betularia), which serves as a quintessential illustration of natural selection in action. Before the onset of the Industrial Revolution, a predominance of light-colored moths existed, allowing them to blend seamlessly with the lichen-covered trees. However, this equilibrium changed dramatically because industrial pollution caused the trees to darken. As a result, darker moths became less discernible to predators; thus, their prevalence within the population increased. This shift in the frequency of dark versus light moths exemplifies natural selection as a response to significant environmental changes (Hof, A. E. V., et al., 2016). Although many might overlook such examples, they reveal the intricate dynamics of adaptation and survival in nature.

5.1. Darwin's Finches: On the Galápagos Islands, Darwin observed that finches displayed distinct beak shapes, which varied according to the types of food available on each island. On islands where hard seeds were common, finches with larger, more robust beaks proved to be more successful at cracking these seeds. However, in contrast, on islands abundant in soft seeds, finches with smaller and more delicate beaks were favored. This variation in beak size serves as a compelling illustration of adaptive radiation and natural selection, primarily driven by ecological niches (Sulloway, 1982).

5.2. Antibiotic Resistance in Bacteria: Within the realm of microorganisms, the swift evolution of antibiotic resistance serves as a striking illustration of natural selection. Bacteria which are subjected to antibiotics that endure—because of mutations that confer resistance—will reproduce, transmitting these resistance traits to subsequent generations. Consequently, this results in increasingly resistant populations of bacteria against medications that were previously effective; however, this presents a notable challenge for medical science. Giraffe Neck Length: The extended necks of giraffes exemplify yet another instance of natural selection. It is posited that giraffes with longer necks could access higher branches (for nourishment), thus bestowing upon them a competitive edge during periods of resource scarcity. As a result, longer necks became more prevalent within the population. Pesticide

Resistance in Insects: Similarly, just as bacteria develop resistance to antibiotics, insects can also acquire resistance to pesticides (Munekage and Kato, 2005)

5.3. Giraffe Neck Length: The extended neck of giraffes serves as a prime example of a key principle of natural selection. It is posited that giraffes with longer necks can access higher foliage for sustenance, thereby granting them a competitive edge during periods of resource scarcity. However, as a result, longer necks become increasingly common within the population (Burkhardt, 2013).

5.4. Pesticide Resistance in Insects: In a manner akin to the evolution of bacterial resistance to antibiotics, insects possess the capacity to develop resistance to pesticides. Over time, those insects that carry genetic mutations rendering them less vulnerable to these chemicals tend to survive and reproduce. This leads to pest populations that present significant challenges to management. This phenomenon has been documented in a plethora of agricultural pests, including (but not limited to) mosquitoes and cockroaches (Hawkins et al., 2018).

Practical examples from the natural world (e.g., the evolution of the peppered moth, Darwin's finches and antibiotic resistance in bacteria) illustrate how natural selection fundamentally shapes species characteristics over time. Understanding these processes is critical for fields ranging from conservation biology to medicine; this insight into how organisms interact with their environments and how species respond to environmental changes is invaluable. However, the implications extend beyond mere observation (because they inform practices that can enhance biodiversity and public health). Although the complexities of these interactions can be daunting, they are essential to grasp.

6. Evolutionary Relationships Between Dinosaurs and Ostrich:

The evolutionary relationship between dinosaurs and ostriches is found within the broad clade of organisms termed avian dinosaurs (commonly known as birds). To elucidate this intricate connection: Dinosaurs and the Genesis of Birds: Birds, in fact, are direct descendants of theropod dinosaurs—a clade that comprises renowned species like T. rex (Tyrannosaurus rex) and Velociraptor. Theropods, characterized by their bipedal stance and carnivorous diet, developed numerous traits akin to those observed in contemporary birds; these traits include feathers, a keeled sternum and an exceptionally efficient respiratory system. Ostriches as Contemporary Avifauna: Ostriches (Struthio camelus) belong to a subgroup of birds classified as ratites (which are sizable, flightless birds possessing flat breastbones) that also encompasses emus, rheas and kiwis. Although ratites do not have the capacity for flight, they are, nevertheless, integral to the broader avian community; this indicates that their evolutionary predecessors were indeed theropod dinosaurs. Common Ancestry: Ostriches, along with other avian species, have a shared ancestor with theropod dinosaurs; however, they embarked on a separate evolutionary trajectory (Ji et al., 2003).)

Fig:1: This picture indicates the morphological similarities between ostrich and dinosaur and clearly narrates the evolutionary relationship between the two. It is the practical example of evolution and natural selection.

This indicates that ostriches are deeply rooted in the extensive avian lineage that can be traced back to dinosaurs. In fact, specific primordial birds, particularly Archaeopteryx, exhibit numerous traits that confirm their connection to theropod dinosaurs. Fig: 1 illustrates a comparative analysis of dinosaurs and ostriches. Key features in common are apparent: ostriches, akin to all avians, display various characteristics linked to their theropod predecessors, including a feathered body (however, ostriches are unable to fly, their plumage serves purposes of insulation and display). They have a hollow, lightweight skeleton tailored for aerial locomotion or, in the case of ostriches, efficient running. Moreover, their three-toed foot also signifies a defining characteristic of certain theropod dinosaurs. In conclusion, ostriches constitute a segment of the modern avian lineage that has directly evolved from theropod dinosaurs. They represent a unique branch of birds that has adapted to a flightless, terrestrial existence; but they still retain numerous hallmark traits of their dinosaur ancestors.

7. Conclusion:

The comprehensive conclusion regarding evolution (as a fundamental biological process) and natural selection reveals intricate dynamics (1) that govern species adaptation. However, one must recognize that practical examples illustrate these principles effectively. Although the theory posits a gradual change, this is not always apparent in observable phenomena. Natural selection operates (2) not merely because of environmental pressures, but also due to genetic variations within populations. These variations can manifest in diverse ways, influencing survival and reproductive success. For instance, the case of the peppered moth exemplifies how coloration confers advantages under specific circumstances, thereby supporting the overarching tenets of evolutionary theory. Thus, the interplay of these factors underscores the complexity of biological evolution, challenging simplistic interpretations. Evolution (1) and natural selection are fundamental concepts in biology; they elucidate the diversity of life on Earth. The examples provided demonstrate the power of natural selection in shaping characteristics of populations over time (2). Understanding evolution is essential for addressing various challenges: antibiotic resistance, climate change and conservation biology. However, this inquiry necessitates a deeper exploration, because the implications of these concepts extend far beyond mere theoretical constructs. Although many grasp the basics, few comprehend the complexity underlying these processes.

References:

1. Burkhardt, R. W. (2013). LaMarck, evolution, and the inheritance of acquired characters. Genetics, 194(4), 793–805. https://doi.org/10.1534/genetics.113.151852
2. Ewens, W. J. (1989). An interpretation and proof of the fundamental theorem of natural selection. Theoretical Population Biology, 36(2), 167–180. https://doi.org/10.1016/0040-5809(89)90028-2
3. Gibbins, I. (2021). Comparative anatomy and evolution of the autonomic nervous system. In Routledge eBooks (pp. 1–67). https://doi.org/10.1201/9781315139807-1

4. Givel, M. (2010). The evolution of the theoretical foundations of punctuated equilibrium theory in public policy. Review of Policy Research, 27(2), 187–198. https://doi.org/10.1111/j.1541-1338.2009.00437.x

5. Hawkins, N. J., Bass, C., Dixon, A., & Neve, P. (2018). The evolutionary origins of pesticide resistance. Biological Reviews, 94(1), 135–155. https://doi.org/10.1111/brv.12440

6. Hendry, A. P., Kinnison, M. T., Heino, M., Day, T., Smith, T. B., Fitt, G., Bergstrom, C. T., Oakeshott, J., Jørgensen, P. S., Zalucki, M. P., Gilchrist, G., Southerton, S., Sih, A., Strauss, S., Denison, R. F., & Carroll, S. P. (2011). Evolutionary principles and their practical application. Evolutionary Applications, 4(2), 159–183. https://doi.org/10.1111/j.1752-4571.2010.00165.x

7. Hof, A. E. V., Campagne, P., Rigden, D. J., Yung, C. J., Lingley, J., Quail, M. A., Hall, N., Darby, A. C., & Saccheri, I. J. (2016). The industrial melanism mutation in British peppered moths is a transposable element. Nature, 534(7605), 102–105. https://doi.org/10.1038/nature17951

8. Ji, Q., Norell, M. A., Makovicky, P. J., Gao, K., Ji, S., & Yuan, C. (2003). An early ostrich dinosaur and implications for ornithomimosaur phylogeny. American Museum Novitates, 3420(1), 1. https://doi.org/10.1206/0003-0082(2003

9. Kolman, W. A. (1960). The mechanism of natural selection for the sex ratio. The American Naturalist, 94(878), 373–377. https://doi.org/10.1086/282139

10. Le, T., Munekage, Y., & Kato, S. (2005). Antibiotic resistance in bacteria from shrimp farming in mangrove areas. The Science of the Total Environment, 349(1–3), 95–105. https://doi.org/10.1016/j.scitotenv.2005.01.006

11. Luna, F., & Moral, P. (1990). Mechanisms of natural selection in human rural populations, survey of a Mediterranean region (La Alpujarra, SE Spain). Annals of Human Biology, 17(2), 153–158. https://doi.org/10.1080/03014469000000902

12. MacConaill, M. A., & Stebbins, G. L. (1972). Processes of organic evolution. Man, 7(1), 148. https://doi.org/10.2307/2799872

13. Osawa, S., Jukes, T. H., Watanabe, K., & Muto, A. (1991). Recent evidence for evolution of the genetic code. In Springer eBooks (pp. 79–95). https://doi.org/10.1007/978-4-431-68302-5_6

14. Selection: The mechanism of evolution. (2008). Choice Reviews Online, 45(11), 45–6139. https://doi.org/10.5860/choice.45-6139

15. Smith, J. M. (1958). The theory of evolution. https://ci.nii.ac.jp/ncid/BA2333487X

16. Sober, E. (2008). Evidence and evolution. https://doi.org/10.1017/cbo9780511806285

17. Sulloway, F. J. (1982). Darwin and his finches: The evolution of a legend. Journal of the History of Biology, 15(1), 1–53. https://doi.org/10.1007/bf00132004

18. Williams, G. C. (2018). Adaptation and natural selection: A critique of some current evolutionary thought. http://ci.nii.ac.jp/ncid/BA04185353

9. ADVANCES IN MUSHROOM CULTIVATION: TECHNIQUES, CHALLENGES AND SUSTAINABLE OPPORTUNITIES

Purvesh B. Bharvad

Botany Department, Pramukh Swami Science and H. D. Patel Arts College, Kadi

E-mail: purveshbot@gmail.com

Abstract:

Mushroom cultivation has undergone transformative advancements, evolving from rudimentary traditional practices to cutting-edge scientific techniques that enhance productivity, efficiency, and sustainability. This review examines the spectrum of methodologies employed in mushroom farming, including substrate optimization, controlled environmental systems, and the integration of biotechnological innovations. It delves into the challenges faced by cultivators, such as climate sensitivity, pest and disease management, and market fluctuations, while offering insights into potential solutions. A focal point of the discussion is the sustainability of mushroom farming, emphasizing its role in promoting circular economies through the utilization of agricultural waste as substrates and its minimal ecological footprint compared to conventional agriculture. Furthermore, the review highlights the significant contribution of mushrooms in addressing global challenges, including food security by providing a protein-rich alternative food source, and waste management through the bioconversion of organic residues. By exploring the intersection of innovation and sustainability, this review underscores the economic and environmental benefits of advancing mushroom cultivation. It advocates for the adoption of progressive strategies and stakeholder collaboration to overcome challenges and unlock the full potential of mushrooms as a sustainable, scalable, and economically viable resource.

Keywords: Mushroom cultivation, Sustainable farming, Bioconversion, Food security, Substrate optimization, Waste management.

1. Introduction:

Mushrooms, belonging to a diverse group of macroscopic fungi, have played an essential role in human culture, diet, and medicine for centuries. Esteemed in cuisines worldwide for their unique flavors and nutritional content, mushrooms are also recognized for their bioactive compounds, which offer a wide range of health benefits. These include anti-inflammatory, antioxidant, and immune-boosting properties, making them a crucial resource for nutraceutical and pharmaceutical industries (Chang & Wasser, 2017). Additionally, mushrooms serve significant ecological roles by decomposing organic matter, recycling nutrients, and fostering soil health.

The global mushroom market has seen consistent growth due to increasing consumer awareness about their health benefits and culinary versatility. As per market data, the global mushroom industry was valued at approximately USD 46 billion in 2020 and is projected to grow at a compound annual growth rate (CAGR) of 9.5% from 2021 to 2028 (Grand View Research, 2021). This surge is driven by urbanization, rising health consciousness, and the growing adoption of mushrooms as a meat alternative in plant-based diets.

Mushroom cultivation has transitioned from small-scale, traditional farming practices to technologically advanced agribusinesses, ensuring higher yields and better quality. Techniques such as controlled environment cultivation, spawn optimization, and the use of enriched substrates have revolutionized the industry. For example, innovations like the use of agricultural and industrial by-products, such as paddy straw, sawdust, and coffee waste as substrates, have enhanced productivity while promoting environmental sustainability (Patra et al., 2020).

Despite these advancements, mushroom cultivation is not without challenges. Issues such as climate sensitivity, pest infestations, and disease outbreaks pose significant risks to production. Moreover, the lack of standardized practices, high initial investment costs, and limited knowledge transfer among small-scale growers hinder widespread adoption. For instance, contamination in spawn production is a major bottleneck in maintaining yield consistency, with studies indicating up to 30% production loss due to pests and pathogens (Ahlawat et al., 2018).

Sustainability has emerged as a critical focal point in mushroom farming. As a resource-efficient crop, mushrooms require less water, land, and energy compared to traditional crops and livestock. Their ability to utilize agricultural waste as a growth substrate exemplifies a circular economy model, reducing environmental footprints while generating additional revenue streams (Ghazala et al., 2021). Furthermore, mushrooms offer promising solutions to global challenges such as food security and waste management. Edible mushrooms, rich in protein, vitamins, and minerals, are increasingly viewed as sustainable alternatives to conventional protein sources.

This review aims to provide a comprehensive exploration of advancements in mushroom cultivation, shedding light on innovative techniques, the challenges faced by growers, and the immense potential of sustainable practices. By understanding these facets, stakeholders can harness the economic and environmental benefits of mushroom farming to meet growing demands while contributing to global sustainability goals.

2. Techniques in Mushroom Cultivation:

2.1. Traditional Methods: Traditional methods of mushroom cultivation have served as the cornerstone for mushroom farming, relying heavily on natural substrates such as logs, compost, and straw. These methods, while labor-intensive and limited in scalability, are well-suited for small-scale farming and regions with abundant natural resources. Scientifically, these practices exemplify the ecological relationship between fungi and their substrates, allowing for the natural decomposition and nutrient recycling that support mushroom growth.

(a). Log Cultivation: Log cultivation is a widely used traditional technique for wood-decomposing mushrooms, particularly Shiitake (*Lentinula edodes*). The process involves inoculating freshly cut hardwood logs (e.g., oak, chestnut) with mushroom spawn. The inoculated logs are sealed with wax to prevent contamination and maintain moisture. These logs are then placed in shaded, moist environments to allow the fungus to colonize and produce fruiting bodies (Royse et al., 2017). This method is low-cost and eco-friendly, leveraging the natural decomposition of lignin and cellulose by the fungal mycelium. However, the long cultivation cycle (6–18 months) and susceptibility to pests, pathogens, and fluctuating environmental conditions pose challenges. Despite these limitations, log cultivation continues to thrive in small-scale and organic farming setups due to its sustainability and minimal reliance on artificial inputs (Chang & Miles, 2004).

(b). Composting: Composting is a traditional yet scientifically robust method for cultivating *Agaricus bisporus* (button mushrooms). The process involves thermophilic decomposition of organic materials such as wheat straw, poultry manure, and gypsum. The preparation of compost occurs in two phases:

> **Phase I - Outdoor Composting:** During this phase, microbial activity generates heat (50–70°C), breaking down complex organic matter into simpler nutrients suitable for fungal growth. This phase lasts 7–14 days, with regular turning and watering to ensure uniform decomposition (Rinker, 2017).

> **Phase II - Pasteurization and Conditioning:** In this phase, the compost is moved to controlled environments, where it undergoes pasteurization at 55–60°C to eliminate

pathogens and competing microorganisms. This step also optimizes the nutrient profile of the compost (Royse et al., 2017).

The use of composting has scientific merit as it utilizes agricultural by-products, contributing to waste recycling and reducing environmental impacts. However, precise control of temperature, aeration, and moisture is critical to avoid contamination and ensure optimal yields. Studies indicate that well-prepared compost can increase yields by up to 40% compared to poorly managed substrates (Zhang et al., 2014).

(c). Straw Cultivation: Straw cultivation is another widely practiced method, particularly for *Pleurotus spp.* (oyster mushrooms). Straw, an agricultural by-product rich in lignocellulosic content, serves as an ideal substrate for fungal colonization. The straw is pre-treated using physical (boiling, steaming) or chemical (lime, formalin) methods to reduce microbial competition (Ahlawat et al., 2011). After sterilization, the treated straw is packed into polythene bags or trays, layered with mushroom spawn, and incubated under dark, humid conditions. The process supports rapid fungal colonization and subsequent fruiting, with oyster mushrooms typically harvested within 3–4 weeks. This technique is cost-effective and widely adopted in developing countries due to its simplicity and reliance on readily available agricultural waste (Singh et al., 2017).

While traditional methods have ecological and economic benefits, they face several scientific and operational challenges:

- **Labor-Intensive Processes:** The preparation and management of natural substrates require significant manual effort, limiting efficiency and scalability.

- **Risk of Contamination:** The lack of sterile conditions and reliance on natural environments increase vulnerability to pests and pathogens, leading to yield losses of up to 30% in some cases (Ahlawat et al., 2011).

- **Extended Cultivation Cycles:** Techniques like log cultivation involve long incubation periods, which are not feasible for large-scale commercial production.

- **Variability in Yields:** Dependence on natural conditions leads to inconsistencies in yield and quality.

From a scientific standpoint, traditional methods highlight the natural symbiosis between fungi and their substrates. Techniques like log and straw cultivation mimic the natural growth conditions of mushrooms, fostering fungal biodiversity and resilience. Composting, on the other hand, represents an advanced biochemical process driven by microbial communities, making it an excellent model for studying microbial ecology and nutrient cycling (Stamets, 2000). The use of agricultural waste as a substrate aligns with circular economy principles, promoting sustainability by converting waste into valuable biomass. However, to meet the growing demand for mushrooms, integrating traditional methods with modern innovations, such as spawn quality enhancement and precision environmental control, is essential.

2.2. Modern Cultivation Techniques: Recent technological advancements have transformed mushroom cultivation, improving efficiency, sustainability, and productivity. Modern cultivation techniques leverage innovations in substrate preparation, environmental control, spawn production and biotechnology to address the limitations of traditional methods and meet increasing global demands.

(a). Substrate Optimization: Substrate optimization is a cornerstone of modern mushroom farming. By using enriched substrates derived from agricultural and industrial by-products, growers can enhance nutrient availability, increase yields, and promote sustainability. Materials such as wheat bran, soybean meal, coffee grounds, and brewery waste are commonly incorporated into substrates to improve their nutritional profile (Patra et al., 2020). For example, studies have shown that adding soybean meal to substrates for *Pleurotus ostreatus* (oyster mushrooms) can boost protein content in the final product while significantly increasing yield (Obodai et al., 2017). Moreover, incorporating lignocellulosic residues, such as sawdust and sugarcane bagasse, not only supports fungal growth but also reduces environmental waste. The ability to recycle organic waste into valuable mushroom biomass aligns with circular economy principles and provides an eco-friendly solution to agricultural by-product disposal.

(b). Controlled Environment Agriculture (CEA): Controlled Environment Agriculture (CEA) has revolutionized mushroom farming by creating precise and automated growing conditions. Automated systems monitor and control critical parameters such as temperature, humidity, carbon dioxide levels, and light intensity to optimize growth and fruiting (Royse et al., 2017). For example, the ideal growing conditions for *Agaricus bisporus* involve maintaining a temperature range of 23–25°C during mycelium colonization and reducing it to 16–18°C during fruiting. Humidity levels above 85% and proper ventilation to maintain CO_2 levels below

1,000 ppm are also critical. Automation reduces human intervention, ensures consistent quality, and minimizes risks of contamination and disease outbreaks (Mata et al., 2018).

CEA systems often utilize sensors, actuators, and IoT-based technology to achieve precision farming. These systems not only enhance productivity but also reduce water and energy consumption, making mushroom farming more sustainable and economically viable (Zhang et al., 2020).

(c). Spawn Production Technology: The quality of spawn is a critical factor in determining the success of mushroom cultivation. Advances in spawn production have shifted from traditional grain-based methods to liquid culture techniques. Liquid culture spawn is produced by growing fungal mycelium in a nutrient-rich liquid medium, ensuring uniform and rapid growth. Liquid spawn production offers several advantages, including higher productivity, reduced contamination risks, and longer shelf life compared to solid spawn. Furthermore, it enables the production of large volumes of high-quality spawn in a shorter time frame, which is essential for commercial-scale farming (Iqbal et al., 2016).

Innovations such as using bioreactors for liquid spawn production have further improved efficiency. Bioreactors provide sterile conditions and precise control over temperature, pH, and aeration, ensuring optimal mycelial growth. This technology is particularly beneficial for large-scale operations, where consistent and reliable spawn is essential for maintaining high yields.

(d). Biotechnology Applications: Biotechnology has opened new frontiers in mushroom cultivation by enabling the development of high-yielding, disease-resistant, and nutritionally enhanced strains. Genetic modification techniques, such as CRISPR-Cas9 and RNA interference (RNAi), have been applied to improve the growth rate, stress tolerance, and bioactive compound production in mushrooms (Liu et al., 2021). For instance, genetic engineering has been used to enhance the production of polysaccharides and secondary metabolites in medicinal mushrooms like *Ganoderma lucidum* and *Cordyceps militaris*, increasing their therapeutic value (Park et al., 2019). Similarly, tissue culture techniques have facilitated the mass propagation of elite mushroom strains with desirable traits.

Another biotechnological advancement is the development of molecular markers for strain identification and quality control. These markers help ensure genetic uniformity and stability in commercial mushroom cultivation, addressing a significant challenge in maintaining consistency across multiple production cycles (Singh et al., 2017). Biotechnology also contributes to sustainable practices by enabling the efficient utilization of waste substrates through enzymatic degradation. For example, ligninolytic and cellulolytic enzymes produced by mushrooms can break down complex agricultural residues into simpler compounds, facilitating their use as substrates (Das & Mukherjee, 2007).

While modern techniques have significantly improved mushroom cultivation, challenges remain. High initial investment costs for CEA systems and biotechnological infrastructure can be a barrier for small-scale farmers. Additionally, regulatory hurdles and public perception issues surrounding genetically modified organisms (GMOs) may limit the adoption of some biotechnological applications. However, the future of mushroom farming lies in integrating traditional knowledge with modern innovations. Research on cost-effective technologies, improved substrate formulations, and environmentally friendly biotechnological solutions will further enhance the scalability and sustainability of mushroom cultivation.

2.3. Emerging Innovations: The mushroom cultivation industry has seen a surge in innovative approaches aimed at addressing challenges such as urbanization, resource scarcity, and the need for sustainable food systems. Emerging innovations like vertical farming and the integration of mushroom cultivation with hydroponics and aquaponics represent groundbreaking advancements that optimize space, improve resource efficiency, and contribute to sustainable agriculture.

(a). Vertical Farming: Vertical farming involves the utilization of vertical space to cultivate mushrooms in stacked layers or shelves, making it particularly suited for urban environments where land availability is limited. This innovation maximizes production per square meter, enabling high-density farming in warehouses, greenhouses, and even indoor facilities within cities. In vertical mushroom farms, controlled environment agriculture (CEA) systems are integrated to maintain optimal conditions such as temperature, humidity, and light. For example, *Pleurotus ostreatus* (oyster mushrooms) and *Lentinula edodes* (shiitake mushrooms) thrive in vertically stacked setups with automated climate control, which reduces human intervention and minimizes errors (Zhang et al., 2020). Vertical farming also offers the advantage of reducing water and energy consumption. By incorporating advanced irrigation systems like misting and drip irrigation, water usage is reduced by up to 70% compared to traditional farming methods (Kalantari et al., 2017). Additionally, the compact design of vertical farms significantly lowers transportation costs and carbon footprints, as production facilities can be situated closer to urban markets. Research has shown that vertical mushroom farming can achieve yields that are 2–3 times higher than conventional horizontal methods while maintaining high-quality produce (Al-Kodmany, 2018). This makes it a promising solution for meeting the rising demand for mushrooms in densely populated areas.

(b). Integration with Hydroponics and Aquaponics: The integration of mushroom cultivation with hydroponic and aquaponic systems is an innovative approach that enhances resource efficiency and promotes circular agriculture. These systems leverage the complementary needs and waste outputs of different organisms, creating symbiotic relationships that maximize productivity.

> ➢ **Hydroponics and Mushrooms:** In hydroponic systems, plants are grown in nutrient-rich water solutions without soil. Mushroom cultivation can be integrated into these systems by using plant waste as a substrate for fungal growth. For instance, the leftover roots, stems, and leaves from hydroponically grown lettuce or spinach can serve as a substrate for *Pleurotus spp.*, thereby reducing agricultural waste (Jensen & Collins, 2021).

This integration not only provides an additional income stream for hydroponic farms but also improves overall sustainability. By converting plant waste into valuable mushroom biomass, hydroponic systems can reduce their environmental footprint while diversifying their agricultural output.

> ➢ **Aquaponics and Mushrooms:** Aquaponics combines aquaculture (fish farming) with hydroponics, where fish waste provides nutrients for plant growth. Mushrooms can further enhance this system by utilizing the organic waste generated by plants and fish. For example, the solid waste from fish tanks can be composted and used as a substrate for mushroom cultivation, creating a closed-loop system (Somerville et al., 2014). Mushrooms like *Agaricus bisporus* and *Pleurotus spp.* have been successfully grown in aquaponic systems, utilizing the nutrient-rich by-products of fish farming. This integration optimizes resource use, reduces waste, and increases the overall productivity of aquaponic farms. Additionally, mushrooms improve the sustainability of aquaponics by breaking down organic matter, which can reduce the accumulation of waste in fish tanks (Kloas et al., 2015).

The integration of mushrooms into vertical farming and hydroponic/aquaponic systems offers several advantages:

- **Space Efficiency:** Vertical farming and hydroponic setups require minimal land, making them ideal for urban and peri-urban areas.
- **Waste Reduction:** Utilizing agricultural and aquaculture waste as substrates for mushrooms promotes circular agriculture and reduces environmental pollution.
- **Economic Diversification:** By incorporating mushroom cultivation, farms can generate additional revenue streams and diversify their product offerings.
- **Environmental Benefits:** These systems significantly reduce water, energy, and land use while minimizing carbon emissions.

Emerging innovations like vertical farming and integration with hydroponics and aquaponics have the potential to transform mushroom cultivation into a highly sustainable and economically viable industry. However, challenges such as high initial setup costs, technical complexity, and the need for skilled labor must be addressed to ensure widespread adoption.

3. Challenges in Mushroom Cultivation:

Mushroom cultivation, despite its rapid growth and potential for profitability, faces several challenges that hinder its scalability, productivity, and sustainability. These challenges are multifaceted, encompassing biological, economic, and logistical issues that require targeted interventions and innovative solutions.

3.1. Pest and Disease Management: One of the most critical challenges in mushroom farming is managing pests and diseases that can cause significant yield losses. Common issues include:

- **Fungal Diseases:** Competing molds such as *Trichoderma spp.* and *Penicillium spp.* frequently contaminate substrates, reducing mushroom yields. These molds outcompete mushroom mycelium for nutrients and space, leading to stunted growth or complete crop failure (Ahlawat et al., 2011).
- **Mites:** Pests like mushroom mites (*Luciaphorus auriculariae*) infest mushroom farms, damaging fruiting bodies and spreading contaminants.
- **Bacterial Infections:** Bacterial blotch caused by *Pseudomonas tolaasii* is a major concern for *Agaricus bisporus* growers, leading to discolored and unmarketable mushrooms.

Effective management strategies involve integrated pest management (IPM), which combines cultural, mechanical, biological, and chemical controls. For example, maintaining proper hygiene, sterilizing substrates, and using disease-resistant strains are critical preventive measures. Biocontrol agents like *Bacillus subtilis* and *Trichoderma harzianum* have shown promise in combating pathogens, providing eco-friendly alternatives to chemical pesticides (Sharma et al., 2020). However, the effectiveness of these measures often depends on the farmer's expertise and the availability of quality biocontrol products.

3.2. Substrate Availability and Quality: Substrate availability and quality are vital for successful mushroom cultivation, as substrates serve as the primary source of nutrients for fungal growth. The heavy reliance on agricultural residues, such as wheat straw, rice husks, sawdust, and corn cobs, poses challenges in regions where these materials are scarce or costly.

- **Regional Limitations:** In areas with limited access to agricultural by-products, growers face difficulties sourcing affordable substrates. For instance, in arid regions, straw availability may be low due to reduced crop production.

- **Contamination Risks:** Substrates of poor quality often harbor contaminants, including competing molds and bacteria, which can compromise mushroom yields. Insufficient pre-treatment of substrates, such as inadequate pasteurization, exacerbates these issues (Zhang et al., 2014).

- **Sustainability Concerns:** The increasing demand for agricultural residues in other industries, such as biofuel production, creates competition and drives up costs for mushroom growers.

To address these challenges, alternative substrates such as industrial by-products (e.g., brewery waste, coffee grounds) and locally available organic materials are being explored. Developing efficient pre-treatment technologies, such as steam pasteurization or chemical sterilization, can also improve substrate quality and reduce contamination risks.

3.3. Market Dynamics: The profitability of mushroom farming is highly influenced by market dynamics, including fluctuations in demand, pricing volatility, and inadequate infrastructure for storage and transportation.

- **Fluctuating Demand:** Consumer demand for mushrooms can be unpredictable, influenced by seasonal preferences, market trends, and competition from other protein-rich foods. For example, gourmet mushrooms like *Lentinula edodes* and *Pleurotus spp.* may experience variable demand compared to more commonly consumed species like *Agaricus bisporus* (Singh et al., 2017).

- **Price Instability:** Price fluctuations due to overproduction, poor market access, or competition with imported mushrooms can significantly impact farmers' profitability.

- **Storage and Transportation Issues:** Fresh mushrooms are highly perishable, with a shelf life of only a few days under ambient conditions. Inadequate cold storage facilities and unreliable transportation networks, especially in developing regions, often result in post-harvest losses of up to 20–30% (Royse et al., 2017).

Addressing market challenges requires investments in cold chain infrastructure, better market forecasting, and the establishment of cooperative networks to improve market access for small-scale farmers. Diversifying into value-added products such as dried mushrooms, mushroom powders, and processed foods can also help stabilize income.

3.4. **Knowledge and Skill Gaps:** The lack of training and technical expertise among farmers, particularly in developing regions, is a significant barrier to adopting advanced mushroom cultivation techniques.

- **Limited Awareness:** Many farmers remain unaware of modern practices such as controlled environment agriculture (CEA), liquid spawn production, and biotechnological innovations.

- **Insufficient Training Programs:** Government and institutional support for training in mushroom farming techniques is often limited, leaving farmers reliant on traditional, less efficient methods.

- **Access to Information:** Poor access to research-based information and technical support further exacerbates the knowledge gap, leading to inconsistent production and quality issues.

Bridging this gap requires capacity-building initiatives, including farmer training programs, demonstration farms, and accessible knowledge-sharing platforms. Collaborative efforts between government agencies, research institutions, and private sector stakeholders can play a pivotal role in disseminating best practices and modern technologies (Kumar et al., 2019).

4. Sustainable Opportunities in Mushroom Cultivation:

Mushroom farming offers numerous sustainable opportunities by addressing environmental challenges, improving public health, and enhancing economic prospects. As a low-input, high-value agricultural enterprise, mushroom cultivation aligns with global efforts toward sustainability and resource optimization.

4.1. Waste Management: One of the most notable sustainable aspects of mushroom farming is its capacity to utilize agricultural and industrial by-products as substrates, effectively reducing waste and promoting circular economy practices. Agricultural residues such as wheat straw, corn cobs, sugarcane bagasse, sawdust, and coffee grounds are rich in lignocellulose, which serves as an excellent nutrient source for fungi. For example, studies have shown that utilizing wheat straw as a substrate for *Pleurotus ostreatus* can result in a 20–30% reduction in agricultural waste (Das & Mukherjee, 2007). Moreover, mushroom cultivation supports the recycling of organic waste generated by industries such as breweries, coffee processing, and paper manufacturing. In addition to reducing waste, the spent mushroom substrate (SMS) left after harvesting can be repurposed as biofertilizer, animal feed, or soil conditioner, further closing the loop in agricultural production (Ghazala et al., 2021). By integrating mushroom farming into waste management systems, growers contribute to reduced landfill use and lower greenhouse gas emissions from organic waste decomposition.

4.2. Nutritional and Medicinal Potential: Mushrooms are highly nutritious, offering significant amounts of protein, dietary fiber, vitamins (B-complex, D), and essential minerals (selenium, potassium, zinc). Additionally, they are low in calories and fat, making them an ideal component of healthy diets. For instance, 100 grams of oyster mushrooms provide approximately 3.3 grams of protein, 2.8 grams of dietary fiber, and substantial amounts of niacin and riboflavin (USDA, 2021). The cultivation of medicinal mushrooms, such as *Ganoderma lucidum* (Reishi) and *Cordyceps militaris*, has opened new opportunities in nutraceuticals and pharmaceuticals. These mushrooms are rich in bioactive compounds, including polysaccharides, triterpenoids, and ergosterol, which have been shown to exhibit antioxidant, anti-inflammatory, and immune-modulating properties (Wasser, 2017). For example, *Ganoderma lucidum* is widely used in traditional medicine to enhance immunity and reduce stress, while *Cordyceps militaris* is valued for its potential in improving respiratory health and athletic performance. The global market for medicinal mushrooms is projected to reach USD 18.9 billion by 2030, reflecting increasing consumer demand for natural health products (Grand View Research, 2022).

4.3. Carbon Sequestration: Fungi, including mushrooms, play a pivotal role in decomposing organic matter, sequestering carbon, and maintaining soil health. During their growth, fungi break down lignocellulose in plant residues, converting it into fungal biomass, which helps store carbon in the form of organic matter (Six et al., 2006). Additionally, mushroom farming reduces methane emissions from decomposing organic waste, as agricultural residues are used as substrates rather than left to decay in landfills. Mycorrhizal fungi, a category of symbiotic fungi, further contribute to carbon sequestration by forming associations with plant roots, enhancing nutrient uptake and stabilizing soil organic carbon. While most edible mushrooms are saprophytic, their overall contribution to the carbon cycle underscores the ecological importance of fungal species. Incorporating mushroom cultivation into agroforestry and regenerative agriculture systems can enhance these benefits, making it a valuable tool in climate change mitigation strategies.

4.4. Livelihood Opportunities: Mushroom cultivation is a labor-intensive activity that generates employment and empowers smallholder farmers, particularly in rural and economically disadvantaged regions. Unlike many agricultural crops, mushrooms can be grown in controlled environments, enabling year-round production and creating consistent income streams for farmers. For instance, a small-scale oyster mushroom farm with an initial investment of USD 1,000 can generate monthly profits ranging from USD 300 to 500, depending on market conditions (Singh et al., 2017). In addition to economic benefits, mushroom farming provides opportunities for marginalized groups, including women and youth, by promoting entrepreneurship and self-reliance. Programs such as India's Directorate of Mushroom Research (DMR) initiatives and the African Mushroom Growers Network have demonstrated the transformative potential of mushroom cultivation in poverty alleviation and rural development (FAO, 2020).

Moreover, the industry's scalability allows for integration into urban settings, where vertical farming and controlled-environment agriculture create employment in densely populated areas. With the global mushroom market projected to grow at a CAGR of 9.5% from 2021 to 2028, the industry presents a growing opportunity for job creation and economic empowerment (Grand View Research, 2021).

5. Conclusion:

Mushroom cultivation represents a unique intersection of tradition and innovation, blending centuries-old practices with modern technological advancements. This dynamic agricultural sector holds immense potential to address some of the most pressing global challenges, including food security, waste management, climate change, and rural development. With their ability to grow on agricultural and industrial by-products, mushrooms exemplify a sustainable approach to farming by promoting circular economy practices and reducing environmental footprints. Despite the significant progress in cultivation techniques, the industry continues to face challenges such as pest and disease management, substrate availability and quality, market dynamics, and knowledge gaps among growers. Addressing these issues requires a concerted effort by policymakers, researchers, and industry stakeholders to provide access to advanced technologies, training programs, and market infrastructure. For instance, investments in integrated pest management (IPM), alternative substrates, and cold storage facilities can significantly enhance productivity and profitability. Moreover, mushrooms offer far-reaching benefits beyond their economic value. They serve as a renewable resource with multifaceted applications, including nutrition, medicine, and environmental sustainability. Edible mushrooms provide high-quality protein and essential nutrients, while medicinal varieties like *Ganoderma lucidum* (Reishi) and *Cordyceps militaris* contribute to the growing nutraceutical and pharmaceutical markets. Their role in carbon sequestration and soil health further underscores their ecological importance, making them a vital component of climate-resilient agricultural systems. Additionally, mushroom farming creates significant livelihood opportunities, particularly in rural and resource-constrained settings. By empowering smallholder farmers, women, and youth through training and capacity-building initiatives, mushroom cultivation can foster economic development and reduce poverty. Urban farming innovations, such as vertical farming and integration with hydroponics and aquaponics, also present new avenues for growth in densely populated areas. As the global demand for mushrooms continues to rise, stakeholders must harness the synergies between tradition and innovation to unlock the full potential of this industry. By adopting sustainable practices, investing in research and development, and improving access to markets and technology, mushroom cultivation can be transformed into a cornerstone of sustainable agriculture and economic resilience. Its adaptability and environmental benefits make mushrooms not only a solution for today's challenges but also a key player in shaping the future of agriculture.

References:

1. Ahlawat, O. P., Gupta, P., & Dhar, B. L. (2011). Innovations in mushroom production for higher productivity and profitability. Indian Journal of Microbiology, 51(3), 245–251.

2. Ahlawat, O. P., Manikandan, K., & Singh, M. (2018). Pest and disease management in mushrooms. Indian Journal of Plant Protection, 46(4), 369–376.

3. Al-Kodmany, K. (2018). The vertical farm: A review of developments and implications for the vertical city. Buildings, 8(2), 24. https://doi.org/10.3390/buildings8020024

4. Chang, S. T., & Miles, P. G. (2004). Mushrooms: Cultivation, nutritional value, medicinal effect, and environmental impact. CRC Press.

5. Chang, S. T., & Wasser, S. P. (2017). The role of culinary-medicinal mushrooms on human welfare with a pyramid model for human health. International Journal of Medicinal Mushrooms, 19(1), 79–85.

6. Das, N., & Mukherjee, M. (2007). Cultivation of Pleurotus ostreatus on weed plants. Bioresource Technology, 98(14), 2723–2726. https://doi.org/10.1016/j.biortech.2006.09.037

7. FAO. (2020). Promoting mushroom farming for poverty alleviation. Food and Agriculture Organization of the United Nations.

8. Ghazala, B., Bhavsar, A., & Nair, S. R. (2021). Mushroom cultivation: An eco-friendly sustainable agriculture practice. Current Science, 120(4), 704–710.

9. Ghazala, B., Bhavsar, A., & Nair, S. R. (2021). Mushroom cultivation: An eco-friendly sustainable agriculture practice. Current Science, 120(4), 704–710.

10. Grand View Research. (2021). Mushroom market size, share & trends analysis report by product, by region, and segment forecasts, 2021–2028.

11. Grand View Research. (2022). Medicinal mushrooms market size, share & trends analysis report, 2022–2030.

12. Iqbal, S. M., Rchman, S. U., & Khalid, A. M. (2016). Recent advances in spawn production for mushroom cultivation. Journal of Mycology, 28(4), 23–32.

13. Jensen, M. H., & Collins, W. L. (2021). Hydroponic systems: Innovations in resource-efficient agriculture. Sustainability in Agriculture, 43(3), 15–29.

14. Kalantari, F., Tahir, O. M., Lahijani, A. M., & Kalantari, S. (2017). A review of vertical farming technology: A guide for implementation and operational decision-making. Agriculture, 7(4), 30. https://doi.org/10.3390/agriculture7040030

15. Kloas, W., Groß, R., Baganz, D., Graupner, J., Monsees, H., Schmidt, U., ... & Wuertz, S. (2015). A new concept for aquaponic systems to improve sustainability, increase productivity, and reduce environmental impacts. Aquaculture Environment Interactions, 7(2), 179–192. https://doi.org/10.3354/aei00146

16. Kumar, S., Singh, M., & Wakchaure, G. C. (2019). Strategies for improving mushroom production: A global perspective. Advances in Horticultural Research, 12(1), 87–100.

17. Liu, H., Pei, Y., & Li, Y. (2021). Advances in the genetic improvement of edible and medicinal mushrooms. Critical Reviews in Biotechnology, 41(3), 1–16. https://doi.org/10.1080/07388551.2020.1863752

18. Mata, G., Savoie, J. M., & Royse, D. J. (2018). Managing environmental conditions for optimum mushroom production. Mushroom Biotechnology, 123–140.

19. Park, Y. J., Baek, S. H., & Hong, S. G. (2019). Enhancing bioactive compound production in medicinal mushrooms. Journal of Biotechnology Advances, 41(5), 18–25. https://doi.org/10.1016/j.biotechadv.2018.10.008

20. Patra, S., Ray, R. C., & Panda, S. K. (2020). Technological advances in edible mushroom cultivation for sustainable food production. Agronomy for Sustainable Development, 40(1), 27. https://doi.org/10.1007/s13593-020-00632-0

21. Patra, S., Ray, R. C., & Panda, S. K. (2020). Technological advances in edible mushroom cultivation for sustainable food production. Agronomy for Sustainable Development, 40, 27.

22. Rinker, D. L. (2017). Handling and composting of organic wastes for mushroom cultivation. Mushrooms: Cultivation, Nutritional Value, Medicinal Effect, and Environmental Impact, 137–145.

23. Royse, D. J., Baars, J., & Tan, Q. (2017). Current overview of mushroom production. In Edible and medicinal mushrooms (pp. 5–13). Wiley Online Library.

24. Sharma, H. S., Bhardwaj, G., & Pathak, A. (2020). Integrated pest management in mushroom cultivation. Journal of Mycology and Plant Pathology, 50(2), 201–210.

25. Singh, M., Vijay, B., Kamal, S., & Wakchaure, G. C. (2017). Mushroom cultivation, marketing and consumption. Directorate of Mushroom Research, Indian Council of Agricultural Research.

26. Singh, M., Vijay, B., Kamal, S., & Wakchaure, G. C. (2017). Mushroom cultivation, marketing and consumption. Directorate of Mushroom Research, Indian Council of Agricultural Research.

27. Six, J., Frey, S. D., Thiet, R. K., & Batten, K. M. (2006). Bacterial and fungal contributions to carbon sequestration in agroecosystems. Soil Science Society of America Journal, 70(2), 555–569. https://doi.org/10.2136/sssaj2004.0347

28. Somerville, C., Cohen, M., Pantanella, E., Stankus, A., & Lovatelli, A. (2014). Small-scale aquaponic food production: Integrated fish and plant farming. FAO.

29. Stamets, P. (2000). Growing gourmet and medicinal mushrooms. Ten Speed Press.

30. USDA. (2021). FoodData Central: Nutritional profile of oyster mushrooms. United States Department of Agriculture.

31. Wasser, S. P. (2017). Medicinal mushrooms in human clinical studies. International Journal of Medicinal Mushrooms, 19(2), 93–108. https://doi.org/10.1615/IntJMedMushrooms.v19.i2.10

32. Zhang, C., Bao, X., & Zhao, X. (2014). Advances in compost substrate preparation and quality control for mushroom cultivation. Compost Science & Utilization, 22(2), 111–122.

33. Zhang, Z., Chen, H., & Wang, L. (2014). Advances in substrate preparation and quality control for mushroom cultivation. Compost Science & Utilization, 22(2), 111–122.

34. Zhang, Z., Chen, H., & Wang, L. (2020). IoT-based environmental monitoring for vertical mushroom cultivation. Computers and Electronics in Agriculture, 178, 105776. https://doi.org/10.1016/j.compag.2020.105776

35. Zhang, Z., Chen, H., & Wang, L. (2020). IoT-based environmental monitoring for mushroom cultivation. Computers and Electronics in Agriculture, 178, 105776. https://doi.org/10.1016/j.compag.2020.105776

10. MOLECULAR BREEDING: BEACON TO COMBAT SALINITY STRESS IN RICE – A REVIEW

Mouli Nahar, Ananya Samanta, Semanti Ghosh*

Department of Biotechnology,

School of Life Sciences, Swami Vivekananda University, Barrackpore, West Bengal – 700121, INDIA.

Corresponding Author's Email: semantig@svu.ac.in, ORCID ID: 0000-0001-8916-5159

Abstract:

This chapter addresses the critical issue of salinity stress in rice cultivation, which affects approximately 800 million hectares worldwide. The problem of salinity, intensified by climate change and inadequate agricultural practices, represents a substantial risk to food security, particularly during the vital growth phases of rice (*Oryza sativa* L.). The study presents a range of strategies aimed at improving salt tolerance in rice, highlighting molecular breeding as a promising avenue for the development of resilient varieties. It discusses the mechanisms underlying salt tolerance, such as ion exclusion and compartmentalization, and examines the genetic diversity found in rice germplasm, including the remarkable tolerance exhibited by wild relatives like *Oryza rufipogon* and *Oryza coarctata*. Furthermore, the chapter evaluates advancements in genetic methodologies, including quantitative trait locus (QTL) mapping, marker-assisted selection (MAS), and genome editing techniques such as CRISPR/Cas9, assessing their contributions to the ongoing development of salt-tolerant rice varieties. In conclusion, the chapter emphasizes that a comprehensive strategy that integrates traditional breeding, modern genomic techniques, and innovative molecular approaches is crucial for ensuring sustainable rice production in areas susceptible to salinity, thereby enhancing global food security.

Keywords: CRISPR/Cas9, MAGIC, MAS, NGS, QTL, SNP Marker, Genetic Modification

1. Introduction:

Salinity presents a significant challenge to rice production worldwide, impacting approximately 800 million hectares of land. Among this, around 45 million hectares of irrigated land are experiencing severe degradation due to salinity issues (Munns 2005; FAO 2008). Several key factors contribute to the rise of salinity in agricultural lands, including insufficient rainfall, which limits the natural leaching of salts from the soil; elevated evaporation rates that exacerbate salt concentration; depletion of groundwater resources, resulting the accumulation of salts in the soil; and poor irrigation practices that fail to manage water effectively (Munns and Gilliham 2015). The situation is further complicated by the impacts of climate emergency, anticipated to intensify both soil salinity and drought conditions. These changes strike a significant threat to postharvest supplies globally, as they can lead to reduced crop yields and compromised agricultural productivity. Rice (*Oryza sativa* L.), a vital staple food primarily cultivated in Asia, is singularly susceptible to the hazardous outcome of salinity stress. This vulnerability is most pronounced during critical growth phases, such as the seedling and reproductive stages, when the plant is the most sensitive to environmental stressors (Chinnusamy et al. 2005; Zeng and Shannon 2000).

The negative consequences of increased salinity on rice cultivation are manifold. Salinity stress takes toll on plant growth, diminishes overall productivity, and can compromise the quality of the grains produced (Thitisaksakul et al. 2015). The primary mechanisms through which salt stress impacts rice plants include ionic imbalance, where the excess salts disrupt the normal ionic composition within plant cells, and the disruption of metabolic functions, which can hinder indispensable physiological processes (Munns and Tester 2008).

To address these challenges, the development of halophytic rice variousness has emerged as a promising strategy. By breeding and engineering rice plants that can withstand higher salinity levels, it becomes possible to cultivate rice in areas that are currently deemed unsuitable due to salinity issues. This approach not only helps maintain productivity in regions affected by salinity but also reduces the need for extensive leaching practices, which can be resource-intensive and environmentally damaging (Munns et al. 2015). Ultimately, the advancement of salt-resistant rice varieties could play a crucial role in ensuring sustainable rice production and enhancing food security in the face of growing environmental challenges.

2. Salt Tolerance Mechanisms:

The accumulation of salt in rice paddies has a considerable effect on rice plants developmental features apposite to crop biomass and productivity. This process of soil salinization hinders plant development by reducing their ability to absorb water and causing cellular damage in the leaves during transpiration, known as osmotic and ion-surplus effects, respectively (Munns 2005). In response to salt stress, rice plants adopt various protective strategies, starting with the exclusion of ions at the root level and progressing to compartmentalization at both the cellular and whole-plant levels. These adaptive strategies can be categorized into three primary types: ion elision, osmoresponsiveness, and tissue endurance (Roy et al. 2014; Reddy et al. 2017).

2.1. Ion Elision in Roots: In the composite interplay between plants and their surrounding environment, the rhizosphere plays an indispensable function, particularly in the management of salt concentrations. It has been observed that approximately 98% of the salt present in the rhizosphere is effectively prevented from entering the plant roots. This remarkable ability allows only trace quantities of salts to traverse the root tissues and subsequently enter the xylem, resulting the transportation of water and nutrients allover the plant system.

The movement of these trace amounts of salts occurs through two primary pathways: the symplastic route and the apoplastic route. The symplastic route involves the movement of substances through the cytoplasm of cells, interconnected by plasmodesmata, while the apoplastic route allows for the movement through the cell walls and intercellular spaces. Despite these pathways being available for salt entry, the plant has evolved specific structural adaptations that significantly limit the influx of salts, particularly sodium ions (Na^+), which can be detrimental to plant health in high concentrations.

One of the key structural impediments to salt movement into the xylem is the presence of the Casparian strips and suberin lamellae located in the endodermis, the innermost layer of the root cortex. The Casparian stripimpregnated with suberin, a waxy substance that creates a hydrophobic barrier. This barrier is crucial in regulating the flow of water and solutes, as it forces all substances entering the vascular system to pass through the selectively permeable cell membranes of the endodermal cells. As a result, this mechanism effectively restricts the passive movement of salts, particularly Na^+, from the root system into the xylem and, consequently, to the aerial parts of the plant. The findings of Das et al. (2015) highlight the importance of these structural adaptations in the endodermis, emphasizing their role in safegaurding plants from the potentially harmful effects of excessive salt accumulation. Through these sophisticated physiological and structural strategies, plants are able to thrive even in challenging conditions, showcasing their remarkable resilience and adaptability.

2.2. Compartmentalization at the Physiological and Cellular Level: In the face of salt stress, a significant challenge for plants, a sophisticated mechanism known as compartmentalization is employed to mitigate the detrimental effects of excess sodium ions (Na^+). This process primarily involves the strategic isolation of harmful Na^+ ions within older leaves and leaf sheaths. As a result, these older tissues become sites of Na^+ accumulation, which accelerates the onset of leaf senescence—essentially, the aging process of leaves. This targeted approach serves a dual purpose: it not only protects the younger, more vital leaves but also preserves the overall health of the plant.

By sequestering Na^+ ions in older leaves, plants effectively reduce the ion concentration in younger leaves, such as flag leaves, which are crucial for photosynthesis and overall plant vigor. This reduction in Na^+ levels in younger tissues is vital for maintaining cellular function and preventing further physiological damage that could arise from high salinity. Additionally, reproductive tissues benefit from this mechanism, as they are critical for the plant's reproductive success and overall yield.

The compartmentalization strategy is particularly important during key growth phases, such as flowering and grain filling, when the demand for photosynthetic activity is at its peak. By ensuring that the rate of leaf production keeps pace with the rate of leaf mortality, plants can maintain adequate photosynthetic capacity. This balance is essential for sustaining energy production and supporting the development of flowers and seeds, ultimately influencing the plant's yield potential.

Studies by Munns (2002) and Negrão et al. (2011) highlight the importance of understanding these physiological mechanisms, as they provide insights into how plants cope with abiotic stressors. The salt tolerance exhibited by rice plants is a complex phenomenon that operates at the cellular level, where individual cells engage in a highly coordinated response to the stress induced by elevated salinity. This response is facilitated through several interrelated mechanisms, including ion elusion, osmotolerance, and tissue endurance, each playing a crucial role in the plant's ability to survive and thrive in saline environments.

At the forefront of these mechanisms is ion exclusion, which primarily involves the transport processes of sodium ions (Na^+) within the root system. This process is essential for limiting the accumulation of harmful Na^+ concentrations in the upper parts of the plant, particularly in the leaves where photosynthesis occurs. The plant employs various strategies to achieve this, such as reducing the movement of Na^+ into the xylem. Additionally, rice plants facilitate the return of Na^+ from the shoots back to the roots, effectively recycling the ions and preventing their toxic buildup in the aerial parts of the plant. Furthermore, the efflux of Na^+ back into the soil is another critical mechanism that helps maintain ion homeostasis and mitigate the detrimental effects of salinity (Negrão et al. 2011; Roy et al. 2014; Ismail and Horie 2017).

In conjunction with ion exclusion, osmotic tolerance takes part in vital function in the plant's response to salt stress. This mechanism is mediated by various sensing molecules, including calcium ions (Ca_2^+), phospholipids, and phytohormones, which work in concert with abscisic acid (ABA) signalling pathways. These pathways are activated in response to osmotic stress, often before any significant accumulation of Na^+ occurs in the shoots. The activation of specific transcription factors is crucial during this phase, as they regulate the expressing genes involved in stress response and acclimatization (Kumar et al. 2013; Reddy et al. 2017). By enhancing osmotic tolerance, rice plants can maintain cellular turgor pressure and metabolic functions even in the presence of high salinity. Tissue tolerance is another critical aspect of salt tolerance in rice plants. This mechanism involves the translocation of Na^+ from the cytoplasm into the vacuoles of older leaves and other structural tissues, effectively sequestering the ions away from sensitive cellular processes. In addition to ion compartmentalization.

2.3. Natural Salt Tolerant Variety Among Rice Germplasm: The success of breeding programs aimed at enhancing salt endurance in rice is significantly influenced by the integration of both traditional and novel genetic variations derived from a diverse array of germplasm. This diversity is crucial for developing resilient rice varieties that can thrive in saline environments, which are becoming increasingly prevalent due to climate crisis and undeveloped agricultural practices (McCouch and Kovach 2008). Numerous studies have highlighted the considerable phenotypic diversity present within rice germplasm, showcasing a bazillionof traits that can be harnessed for breeding purposes. For instance, Quijano-Guerta and Kirk (2002), Negrão et al. (2011), De Leon et al. (2015), and Sakina et al. (2016) have all documented variations in salt tolerance among different rice varieties, emphasizing the potential for selecting and breeding for improved salinity resistance.

Generally, indica rice varieties have been observed to exhibit greater resilience to salt stress compared to their *japonica* counterparts. This enhanced tolerance is often attributed to their superior physiological mechanisms, which include the ability to effectively exclude sodium ions, enhance potassium uptake, and maintain a favourable sodium-to-potassium (Na^+/K^+) ratio in plant tissues (Lee et al. 2003b). Such mechanisms are critical for sustaining cellular functions and overall plant health under saline conditions.

Among the rice varieties recognized for their exceptional salinity tolerance are "Pokkali" and "Nona Bokra." These varieties are not only important genetic resources for breeding programs but also demonstrate remarkable adaptability to coastal saline conditions, making them invaluable for farmers in affected regions. In addition to these well-known varieties, several local strains and cultivars exhibiting moderate to high salinity tolerance have been identified and cultivated in salinity-prone areas.

Research efforts have also focused on exploring the genetic diversity within wild rice species. For example, Mishra et al. (2016) conducted an evaluation of Indian wild rice germplasm and identified two lines with high salt tolerance, fourteen with moderate tolerance, and twenty-eight with varying levels of tolerance. These lines were primarily sourced from *Oryza rufipogon* and *Oryza nivara*, highlighting the potential of wild lineage in contributing to the genetic pool for salt endurance.

The development of the salt-tolerant rice line DJ15 represents a key advancement in agricultural biotechnology, achieved through the hybridization of a wild rice line, *Oryza rufipogon*, specifically the Dongxiang variety, with a japonica cultivar known as Ninjing 16. This innovative breeding approach aimed to enhance the resilience of rice crops to saline environments, which are becoming increasingly prevalent due to climate crisis and rising sea levels.

In a more recent investigation conducted by Prusty et al. (2018), researchers identified seven wild rice accessions that exhibited remarkable levels of salt tolerance comparable to those found in well-known salt-tolerant varieties such as Pokkali, Nona Bokra, and FL478. The wild species studied included *Oryza alta, Oryza latifolia, Oryza coarctata, Oryza rhizomatis, Oryza eichingeri, Oryza minuta,* and *Oryza grandiglumis*. These accessions demonstrated significant tissue tolerance to salinity stress, which is crucial for maintaining plant health and productivity in saline conditions. Notably, they were able to preserve chlorophyll content in their young leaves, an indicator of their ability to maintain photosynthetic efficiency even under adverse conditions.

Among these wild rice species, *Oryza coarctata* stands out due to its unique adaptation to saline environments. This salt marsh species, native to the eastern coast of India, has shown an impressive capacity to endure salinity levels ranging from 20 to 40 dS m^{-1}, and in some cases, even higher concentrations, without suffering from detrimental effects. This remarkable tolerance was highlighted in the work of Sengupta and Majumder (2010), who emphasized the potential of *O. coarctata* as a valuable genetic resource for breeding programs aimed at developing new rice varieties that can thrive in saline soils.

The findings from these studies underscore the importance of exploring wild rice species as a source of genetic diversity for amplifying salt resistant in cultivated rice. By leveraging the natural adaptations of these wild relatives, researchers and breeders can develop new cultivars that are better equipped to cope with the challenges posed by salinity, ultimately contributing to food security in regions affected by saline conditions.

3. Conventional Approaches to Enhance Salinity Tolerance Breeding: Conventional and Mutational:

Traditional plant breeding is a well-established approach for enhancing the genetics of various crop species by merging desirable traits. In rice cultivation, different selection techniques have been utilized to boost salt tolerance. However, developing salt-tolerant rice varieties through conventional breeding poses significant challenges, particularly in pinpointing the most relevant physiological traits linked to salt endurance and the involvement of multiple genetic factors (Fita et al. 2015). Several salt-tolerant rice varieties have emerged from local and traditional salt-resistant cultivars, which have been commercialized in several Asian countries, including Bangladesh, India, and the Philippines (Ismail and Horie 2017).

For instance, the salinity-tolerant varieties CSR-1, CSR-2, and CSR-3 were developed through pure line selection from local cultivars in India. Likewise, varieties such as SR-26B, Hamilton, Patnai-23, and Jhona-349 were created through site-specific selection in various countries, leveraging enhanced genetic backgrounds via recombination breeding (Gregorio et al. 2002). The International Rice Research Institute (IRRI) employed a shuttle-breeding strategy to produce the salt-tolerant varieties CSR23 and CSR27 (Mishra 1994). Additionally, CSR36, which exhibited salinity tolerance during the vegetative stage, was released in India, while Binadhan 10, which showed tolerance at the reproductive stage, was introduced in Bangladesh (Ismail and Horie 2017). Despite the achievements of conventional breeding methods, challenges persist in developing high-yielding rice varieties that also demonstrate improved salt tolerance. Many salt-tolerant cultivars often exhibit suboptimal agronomic traits, such as low production, abnormal height, and sensitivity to photoperiod (Reddy et al. 2014). The intricate nature of the physiological traits affecting salt tolerance further complicates these challenges.

Mutation breeding is a highly effective method for developing rice varieties that are both salt-tolerant and high-yielding, especially since it raises fewer ethical concerns than transgenic methods (Das et al. 2014). This approach is particularly useful for enhancing existing cultivars that may lack certain desirable traits, such as resistance to salt. The use of ionizing radiation—including gamma rays, X-rays, neutrons, and various chemical mutagens—has been widely recognized as a reliable way to induce mutagenesis. Numerous studies have demonstrated that mutagenesis can significantly increase genetic diversity related to salinity tolerance in rice. Notable salt-tolerant varieties, such as Shua 92 (Mustafa et al. 1997) and Basmati 370 (Saleem et al. 2005), have been developed using gamma irradiation techniques. Additionally, Takagi et al. (2015) identified a loss-of-function mutation linked to salt tolerance, which resulted in the creation of a salt-tolerant variety named "Kaijin." Moreover, rice seeds treated with carbon and neon ions have yielded a mutant variety with enhanced salt tolerance (Hayashi et al. 2007). The NIAB Rice-1 and PSR 1-84 varieties, developed through gamma radiation, have demonstrated improved yields under saline conditions compared to established salt-tolerant varieties like Pokkali and Johna 349 (Anonymous 1986). Similarly, chemical mutagenesis has been employed to boost salinity tolerance in rice. A specific salt-tolerant mutant, known as rst1, was identified from an ethyl-methanesulfonate (EMS) mutant library, showing notable elevated chlorophyll content and shoot biomass, along with decreased electrolyte leakage and lipid peroxidation under salinity stress (Deng et al. 2015).

3.1. Tissue Culture: Tissue culture methodologies are essential for speeding up the development of rice breeding lines that can withstand abiotic stresses (Zhang et al. 2014). By using double haploid technology, the time required to create homozygous and uniform breeding lines can be reduced by about five to seven years compared to traditional breeding methods (Germana 2011). The success of anther culture depends on several factors, including the genotype of the donor plant, the developmental stage of the microspores, the use of cold treatment, and the composition of the induction and differentiation media. Indica rice varieties typically show lower rates of callus induction and regeneration, which poses a challenge for breeding double haploid lines (Cha-um et al. 2009). Atabaki et al. (2018) were able to produce salt-tolerant lines from the Malaysian rice cultivar MR263 through somatic embryogenesis, using culture media supplemented with 100–300 mM NaCl to create salt-tolerant calli and regenerants. Additionally, inducing somaclonal variation in the rice cultivar Wagwag led to the development and release of the moderately salinity-tolerant variety Salinas 14 in the Philippines (Ismail and Horie 2017). The combination of in vitro mutagenesis, which merges in vitro culture with physical mutagens, has proven effective in increasing genetic diversity and promoting the development of crops, including rice, that can tolerate abiotic stresses (Lee et al. 2003a). Various tissue culture techniques have successfully produced salt-tolerant lines that are well-adapted for cultivation in saline-prone rice-growing regions. The improved lines generated through tissue culture hold significant promise as donors for salt tolerance in a variety of ancestry pedigree.

4. Molecular Approaches to Enhance Salinity Tolerance:

4.1. QTL: The mapping of quantitative trait loci (QTL) has significantly enhanced our comprehension of the genetic determinants associated with salt tolerance. Predominantly, QTL studies have employed recombinant inbred lines (RIL), doubled haploid (DH), or introgression lines (IL) as their foundational mapping populations. A multitude of studies has pinpointed various QTLs associated with traits of salt tolerance, notably the Saltol QTL located on chromosome 1, which is responsible for 43% of the phenotypic variation concerning the Na^+/K^+ ratio and salinity tolerance during the seedling phase (Bonilla et al., 2002). Subsequent research conducted by Thomson et al. (2010) investigated the Saltol locus within a RIL population derived from IR29 and Pokkali, elucidating its function in the regulation of Shoot Na^+/K^+ homeostasis. Additional noteworthy QTLs include SKC1 on chromosome 1 and qSNC7 on chromosome 7, which account for 40.1% and 48.5% of the phenotypic variance, respectively, suggesting the participation of distinct genes in the transport of Na^+ and K^+ (Lin et al., 2004). Ren et al. (2005) validated the qSKC1 locus as a sodium transporter crucial for maintaining K^+ homeostasis under saline conditions. Furthermore, Bimpong et al. (2013) identified seven significant QTLs associated with root length, plant height, and shoot weight through the utilization of 384 SNP markers in a RIL population derived from IR29 and Hasawi.

Sixteen quantitative trait loci (QTLs) linked to salinity tolerance during the seedling phase were identified in a recombinant inbred line (RIL) population from the Bengal and Pokkali cross, using a SNP linkage map from genotyping-by-sequencing (De Leon et al., 2016). Gimhani et al. (2016) found 83 QTLs related to 11 morpho-physiological traits for salinity tolerance in another RIL population from At354 and Bg352, explaining 12.5% to 46.5% of phenotypic variation, with most clustered in 14 genomic regions. Bizimana et al. (2017) reported 20 novel QTLs for salinity traits on chromosomes 1, 2, 4, 6, 8, and 9 in a RIL population from Hasawi x IR29, noting that Hasawi lacks salinity tolerance alleles found in Nona Bokra and Pokkali. This study revealed overlapping QTL regions on chromosomes 1, 4, 6, 8, and 12, indicating potential new salt-immune alleles in Hasawi (Rahman et al., 2017). However, research on salinity tolerance genetics during the reproductive stage in rice is limited. Additionally, 35 QTLs for yield traits were identified in an F2 population from Sadri and FL478, with 28 accounting for 6% to 30% of phenotypic variation (Mohammadi et al., 2013). Hossain et al. (2015) identified 16 quantitative trait loci (QTLs) that accounted for 4% to 47% of the phenotypic diversity across chromosomes 1, 7, 8, and 10 in an F2 mapping population created from a cross between the salt-immune donor Cherivirupu and Pusa Basmati 1 (PB1). The study indicated that the concentration of sodium ions (Na^+), pollen fertility, and the Na^+/K^+ ratio in the flag leaf are critical factors contributing to salinity tolerance during the reproductive stage. Furthermore, the implementation of a bulk segregant analysis in a recombinant inbred line (RIL) population derived from "CSR11/MI48" having three QTLs associated with salt resistance at the reproductive stage, specifically linked to grain yield (Tiwari et al. 2016).

Chromosome segment substitution lines (CSSLs) and introgression line (IL) populations are vital for mapping quantitative trait loci (QTLs) and discovering associated genes (Ali et al. 2010; Thuy et al. 2018). An IL population derived from the salt-tolerant donors Pokkali and Nona Bokra has been instrumental in identifying QTLs related to seedling salinity in rice. De Leon et al. (2017) identified 18 and 32 QTLs using SSR and SNP markers, respectively, in a Pokkali IL population in the "Bengal" background, confirming 14 previously established QTLs. Puram et al. (2017) found 33 additive QTLs in an IL population with Nona Bokra in the "Jupiter" background, while another study identified 32 QTLs in the Cheniere background, suggesting that mechanisms like Na^+/K^+ homeostasis and Na^+ exclusion contribute to Nona Bokra's salt tolerance (Puram et al. 2018).

Nounjan et al. (2016) evaluated two Chromosome Segment Substitution Lines (CSSLs) of the KDML105 rice variety, which included drought tolerance segments (DT-QTL8), and found improved tolerance to drought and salinity. Chutimanukul et al. (2018) reported that CSSL16, derived from KDML105, showed greater salinity tolerance than KDML05, identifying ten significant genes, with PsbS1 as a key candidate for maintaining photosynthetic function under salinity stress. Thuy et al. (2018) used CSSLs with tolerance segments from Nona Bokra in a salt-sensitive Koshihikari background to explore salinity tolerance mechanisms, linking specific chromosomal regions to the exclusion of Na^+ and Cl^- ions.

The genome-wide association study (GWAS) is a key method for investigating the genetic basis of quantitative traits in rice, particularly regarding abiotic stresses like salinity. A study of 180

European japonica accessions identified 14 quantitative trait loci (QTLs) and 65 candidate genes for salinity tolerance, suggesting at least nine beneficial alleles are necessary for improved salt tolerance through marker-assisted breeding (Ahmadi et al. 2011). Kumar et al. (2015) found 64 SNPs linked to salt stress and Na^+/K^+ ratios, while Shi et al. (2017) identified 22 significant SNPs associated with salinity tolerance. Batayeva et al. (2018) reported 26 QTLs for seedling salinity stress, with 11 corresponding to known salt-tolerance genes. Frouin et al. (2018) evaluated 235 temperate *japonica* accessions using 30,000 SNPs, finding significant QTLs near genes involved in calcium signaling. Cui et al. (2018) conducted six multi-locus GWAS on germination under salinity stress, analyzing 478 accessions and 162,529 SNPs, identifying 371 quantitative trait nucleotides (QTNs) and 66 candidate genes. Yu et al. (2017) discovered 93 candidate genes linked to salinity tolerance in 295 accessions. Naveed et al. (2018) identified 20 QTNs related to 11 salinity-influenced traits during germination and seedling phases, using 395,553 SNP markers across 208 accessions. Lekklar et al. (2019) examined salinity tolerance at flowering in 104 Thai rice accessions, uncovering 448 SNPs across 200 loci, with 73% overlapping known QTLs. An et al. (2019) identified 54 QTLs related to salt tolerance in 181 cultivars, highlighting 17 loci associated with seedling dry weight.

4.2. MAS: Marker-assisted selection (MAS) enhances traditional breeding by using DNA markers for indirect selection, facilitating the development of salt-tolerant cultivars. While MAS is straightforward for qualitative traits, it poses challenges for complex polygenic traits like salinity stress tolerance (Ashraf et al. 2012). This technique accelerates breeding cycles by recovering recurrent genomes in fewer generations. Successful introgression of salt tolerance quantitative trait loci (QTLs), particularly the "Saltol" QTL, has been achieved in high-yielding rice varieties through marker-assisted backcrossing (MABC). Notable examples include PB1121, PB6, AS996, Bac Thom 7, BRRI dhan49, and various local varieties in India (Singh et al. 2016b).

Punyawaew et al. (2016) used marker-assisted backcrossing to incorporate the Saltol QTL into the Thai rice variety KDM105, resulting in introgression lines (ILs) with improved survival, reduced sodium absorption, and enhanced potassium uptake, highlighting the "Saltol" gene's role in Na^+/K^+ balance. Similarly, near-isogenic lines (NILs) with "Saltol" introduced into "IR64" (Ho et al. 2016), "Pusa Basmati" (Singh et al. 2018b), and "Improved White Ponni" (Valarmathi et al. 2019) also showed better salinity tolerance. Recently, Rana et al. (2019) transferred the hst1 salinity-tolerance gene from the salt-resistant "Kaijin" to the high-yielding "Yukinko-mai" using marker-assisted selection and speed-breeding, creating the salinity-tolerant population "YNU21-2-4," which exhibited significant tolerance during both seedling and reproductive stages.

The effectiveness of MAS for improving salt tolerance is influenced by trait heritability, the number and impact of QTLs, and population size. Most QTLs, aside from Saltol, have minimal effects and are affected by environmental conditions. Challenges include high costs and broad confidence intervals for QTLs, complicating the introgression of desired traits due to linkage drag. Therefore, advancements are needed to enhance the reliability and cost-effectiveness of MAS for developing salt-tolerant rice varieties.

4.3. Genetic Modification: The successful application of genetic modification techniques in developing salt-tolerant plants has been achieved through the overexpression or introduction of specific genes into toplandraces. Given the well-established role of antioxidants, osmo-protectants, ion transport, and various transcription factors in salt tolerance, these elements have been primarily utilized in genetic engineering approaches to enhance salinity tolerance in rice (Ashraf et al. 2008). A substantial body of transgenic research has been conducted to improve salt tolerance in rice using genes from diverse sources, as reviewed by several authors (Bajaj and Mohanty 2005; Kathuria et al. 2007; Hoang et al. 2016; Reddy et al. 2017).

The most recent studies employing transgenic strategies to enhance salinity tolerance. Notably, the transgenic pyramiding of salt-responsive protein 3-1 (SaSRP3-1) and vacuolar H^+-ATPase subunit c1 (SaVHAc1) has demonstrated improved salt tolerance during both seedling and reproductive stages (Biradar et al. 2018) (TABLE 1).

Additionally, research has highlighted the significant role of RING E3 ligases in salinity tolerance. For example, elevated transcript levels of OsRMR1 (Lim et al. 2015) and OsSIRP2 (Chapagain et al. 2018) were observed under salinity stress conditions, resulting in enhanced salinity tolerance in transgenic *Arabidopsis*. However, these findings necessitate further validation in rice. The development of salinity-tolerant rice through genetic engineering has been hindered by several factors, including insufficient knowledge of major genes contributing to salinity endurance, inadequate transgene expression or silencing, and public resistance to genetic modification approaches. To advance this field, future research should focus on targeting multiple genes involved in various salt-tolerance mechanisms, utilizing stress-inducible promoters to enhance overall salt resistance.

Table 1. List of genes from different organisms and their functions

Organism	Gene	Function	Ref
Antirrhinum majus	*AmRosea1*	Increased activity of potassium transporters and catalase.	Dou et al. (2017)
Eleusine coracana L	*EcNAC67*	Transgenic plants have longer roots and shoots and show less biomass decline than non-transgenic plants.	Rahman et al. (2016)
O. sativa	*OsMYB6*	Elevated levels of reactive oxygen species quenchers and proline concentration.	Tang et al. (2019)
O. sativa	*OsGS1;1 and OsGS2*	Increased grain production and enhanced photosynthetic efficiency	James et al. (2018)
O. sativa	*STRK1*	The activation of CatC, a member of a protein family that diminishes hydrogen peroxide levels	Zhou et al. (2018)
O. sativa	*OsSta2*	Enhanced chlorophyll concentration and improved grain production	Kumar et al. (2017)
O. sativa	*OsPP1a*	An elevated germination rate, increased kernel weight, and enhanced levels of ascorbate peroxidase and superoxide dismutase have been observed	Liao et al. (2016)
O. sativa	*ONAC022*	The reduction in Na$^+$ concentration is	Hong et al. (2016)

		associated with an enhancement in both root and shoot length	
O. sativa	*OsHNX1*	Reduced leaf damage score and increased chlorophyll content; enhanced spikelet fertility and grain yield.	Amin et al. (2016)
Populus trichocarpa	*PtCYP714A3*	Enhanced expression of the NHX1 and SOS1 genes.	Wang et al. (2016)

5. Innovative Tools for Molecular Breeding:

5.1. Approach of MAGIC: The multi-parental advanced generation intercross (MAGIC) methodology has been used for QTL mapping of traits related to abiotic stress tolerance. This approach intercrosses various founder lines, including contemporary and traditional varieties with key agronomic traits like grain productivity, calibre, and salinity resilience (Bandillo et al. 2013). As a result, the MAGIC population features elite lines with valuable agro-morphological traits, aiding in gene discovery and rice variety improvement. Bandillo et al. (2013) created new MAGIC rice populations, including "*indica*" MAGIC with eight indica parents, MAGIC plus with eight indica parents from two rounds of inter-crossing, *japonica* MAGIC with eight *japonica* parents, and Global MAGIC combining eight parents from each *indica* and *japonica* group respectively. They mapped QTLs for bothabiotic and biotic stresses, finding salt tolerance in a subset of S4 lines from the indica MAGIC population, with significant markers on chromosome 1 between 9.2 and 12 Mb, near the SALT, qSKC-1, and Saltol QTLs. Salinity endurance in 970 selected MAGIC *indica* lines, identifying 36 lines with moderate to high salt tolerance through morpho-physiological assessment and SSR evaluation (Samaco et al., 2018).

5.2. Genomic Selection, NGS and Gene Editing: Advancements in next-generation sequencing (NGS) have lowered sequencing costs, enabling the use of thousands of genetic markers in genomic selection to enhance quantitative traits (Breseghello and Guedes 2013). This strategy identifies superior individuals using genome-wide DNA markers, improving breeding efficiency for traits like salt tolerance by estimating individual breeding values from extensive marker data, unlike traditional marker-assisted selection (MAS) (Bhandari et al. 2019).

Intensive SNP markers and rice genome sequencing facilitate the detection of numerous QTLs (Grenier et al. 2015). Genomic estimated breeding values (GEBVs) are calculated from statistical models that integrate phenotypic and genotypic data from a training population to predict breeding performance (Bhat et al. 2016). Selection relies on the allelic composition of markers linked to phenotypic traits in the training population (Spindel and Iwata 2018). Genomic selection also enables performance predictions across generations, as shown by Wang et al. (2017b) in hybrid rice using the GBLUP model.

Various transcriptome-profiling methods exist for identifying differentially expressed genes in reaction to abiotic stressoras salinity (Subudhi 2011; Bansal et al. 2013). Among these, next-generation sequencing (NGS)-based RNA sequencing (RNA-Seq) has become a leading tool for global expression profiling due to its cost-effectiveness and accurate transcript quantification (Oono et al. 2011). This method allows for detailed monitoring of transcript expression changes over time and across treatments, as well as the study of post-transcriptional modifications and alternative splicing (Shelden and Roessner 2013). Comparative analyses show that the salt-immune line FL478 has more effective mechanisms for signal transduction and potassium transport than the susceptible line IR29 (Mansuri et al. 2019). Additionally, tolerant *japonica* cultivars activate genes related to signal translation and salt stress responses earlier than susceptible ones (Formentin et al. 2018). Shankar et al. (2016) identified salinity response transcripts in the tolerant rice cultivar Pokkali, which may help discover new salt-tolerance genes. Wang et al. (2017) found that only 286 of 5273 differentially expressed genes came from the salt-tolerant *indica* parent in their comparative transcriptomic analysis. The accumulation of genomic resources, such as SNPs, InDels, and differentially expressed genes, will enhance our understanding of salt tolerance mechanisms and aid in identifying related genes and QTLs, accelerating the development of salt-resistant rice varieties.

Unlike mutation breeding, which causes random mutations across the genome, genome editing targets specific sites for alteration. Techniques like homing endonucleases (HEs), zinc finger nucleases (ZFNs), TALENs, and CRISPR/Cas9 use site-specific nucleases (SSNs) to create double-stranded breaks (DSBs) in DNA. These DSBs can be repaired via homology-dependent recombination (HDR) or nonhomologous end-joining (NHEJ). HDR uses a homologous DNA template for repair, while NHEJ often leads to random insertions and deletions, potentially causing frameshift mutations. CRISPR/Cas9 stands out for its simplicity and ability to target multiple sites simultaneously, utilizing a 20-nucleotide guide RNA and a 5′-NGG protospacer adjacent motif (PAM) recognized by the Cas9 enzyme to create DSBs, which are then repaired through HDR or NHEJ. This combination allows for precise genomic targeting.

 CRISPR/Cas-generated mutant variant of the OsRR22 gene showed enhanced salt tolerance in seedlings (Zhang et al. 2019). The CRISPR/Cas system has also helped identify salt-tolerant genes like OsNECD3 (Huang et al. 2018), OsNAC041 (Wang et al. 2019), and the GT-1 element of OsRAV2 (Duan et al. 2016). Despite being a newer tool, genome editing is favoured for its precision in modifying specific genomic regions without adding exogenous genes. However, challenges include low efficiency of homology-directed repair (HDR) and potential off-target mutations, while it allows for simultaneous manipulation of multiple genes.

6. Conclusion:

Improving rice for salinity tolerance is vital for global food security, as salt stress adversely impacts growth and yield. The genetic complexity of salinity tolerance, involving multiple protective mechanisms, poses a challenge. However, advancements in genomics offer opportunities to enhance this trait. MAS, the key strategy for developing salt-tolerant rice varieties by targeting tolerance traits. Molecular breeders will focus on identifying and combining quantitative trait loci (QTLs) linked to salt resilience. Next-generation sequencing tools like MutMap, QTL-Sequence, RNA-Sequence, and GBS will aid in understanding the genetic basis of salt tolerance. While various salt-tolerant varieties exist, the specific mechanisms of tolerance in these resources are not fully understood. No single variety has all necessary mechanisms, indicating a need for further research to catalogue these traits and accumulate desirable alleles. Genomic tools can also helpadvantageous alleles for salt tolerance from natural genetic resources. Gene editing technology presents a propitious method for developing de novo gene variants associated with salt tolerance. Ultimately, a better understanding of these mechanisms, along with advancements in genotyping and phenotyping, will enhance breeding programs for high-yielding, salt-tolerant rice varieties.

References:

1. Abe, A., Kosugi, S., Yoshida, K. et al. (2012). Genome sequencing reveals agronomically important loci in rice using MutMap. Nat. Biotechnol. 30: 174–178.

2. Ahmadi, J. and Fotokian, M.H. (2011). Identification and mapping of quantitative trait loci associated with salinity tolerance in rice (*Oryza sativa*) using SSR markers. Iran. J. Biotechnol. 9: 21–30.

3. Ahmadi, N., Negrão, S., Katsantonis, D. et al. (2011). Targeted association analysis identified japonica rice varieties achieving Na$^+$/K$^+$ homeostasis without the allelic make-up of the salt tolerant indica variety Nona Bokra. Theor. Appl. Genet. 123: 881–895.

4. Ahmed, A.U., Hernandez, R., and Naher, F. (2016). Adoption of stress-tolerant rice varieties in Bangladesh. In: Technological and Institutional Innovations for Marginalized Smallholders in Agricultural Development (eds. F. Gatzweiler and J. von Braun). Cham, Springer https://doi .org/10.1007/978-3-319-25718-1_15.

5. Akbar, M., Yabuno, T., and Nakao, S. (1972). Breeding for saline-resistant varieties of rice. Jpn. J. Breed. 22: 277–284.

6. Ali, M.L., Sanchez, P.L., Yu, S. et al. (2010). Chromosome segment substitution lines: a powerful tool for the introgression of valuable genes from Oryza wild species into cultivated rice (O. sativa). Rice 3: 218.

7. Amin, U.S.M., Biswas, S., Elias, S.M. et al. (2016). Enhanced salt tolerance conferred by the complete 2.3 kb cDNA of the rice vacuolar Na+/H+ antiporter gene compared to 1.9 kb coding region with 5'UTR in transgenic lines of rice. Front. Plant Sci. 7: 14.

8. Ammar, M.H.M., Pandit, A., Singh, R.K. et al. (2009). Mapping of QTLs controlling Na$^+$, K$^+$ and CI$^-$ ion concentrations in salt tolerant indica rice variety CSR27. J. Plant. Biochem. Biotechnol. 18: 139–150.

9. An, H., Liu, K., Wang, B. et al. (2019). Genome-wide association study identifies QTLs conferring salt tolerance in rice. Plant Breed. 139: 73–82. https://doi.org/10.1111/pbr.12750.

10. Ashraf, M. (1994). Breeding for salinity tolerance in plants. Crit. Rev. Plant Sci. 13: 17–42.

11. Ashraf, M., Akram, N.A., Rahman, M.U., and Foolad, M.R. (2012). Marker-assisted selection in plant breeding for salinity tolerance. Methods Mol. Biol. 913:305–333.

12. Ashraf, M., Athar, H.R., Harris, P.J.C., and Kwon, T.R. (2008). Some prospective strategies for improving crop salt tolerance. Adv. Agron. 97: 45–110.

13. Atabaki, N., Nulit, R., Kalhori, N. et al. (2018). In vitro selection and development of Malaysian salt tolerant rice (Oryza sativa L. cv. MR263) under salinity. Acta Sci. Agric. 2: 8–17.

14. Bajaj, S. and Mohanty, A. (2005). Recent advances in rice biotechnology towards genetically superior transgenic rice. Plant Biotechnol. J. 3: 275–307.

15. Bandillo, N., Raghavan, C., Muyco, P.A. et al. (2013). Multi-parent advanced generation inter-cross (MAGIC) populations in rice: progress and potential for genetics research and breeding. Rice 6: 1–15.

16. Bansal, K.C., Lenka, S.K., and Mondal, T.K. (2013). Genomic resources for breeding crops with enhanced abiotic stress tolerance. Plant Breed. 133: 1–11.

17. Batayeva, D., Labaco, B., Ye, C. et al. (2018). Genome-wide association study of seedling stage salinity tolerance in temperate japonica rice germplasm. BMC Genet. 19: 2.

18. Bhandari, A., Bartholome, J., Cao-Hamadoun, T.-V. et al. (2019). Selection of trait-specific markers and multi-environment models improve genomic predictive ability in rice. PLoS ONE 14: e02008871.

19. Bhat, J.A., Ali, S., Salgotra, R.K. et al. (2016). Genomic selection in the era of next generation sequencing for complex traits in plant breeding. Front. Genet. 7: 221.

20. Bimpong, I.K., Manneh, B., El-Namaky, R. et al. (2013). Mapping QTLs related to salt tolerance in rice at the young seedling stage using 384-plex single nucleotide polymorphism SNP marker sets. Mol. Plant Breed. 5: 47–63.

21. Biradar, H., Karan, R., and Subudhi, P.K. (2018). Overexpression of a salt responsive protein3-1 (SaSRP3-1) as well as pyramiding with SaVHAc1 from Spartina alterniflora L. enhances salt tolerance in rice. Front. Plant Sci. 9: 1304.

22. Bizimana, J.B., Luzi-Kihupi, A., Murori, R.W., and Singh, R.K. (2017). Identification of quantitative trait loci for salinity tolerance in rice (Oryza sativa L.) using IR29/Hasawi mapping salinity population. J. Genet. 96: 571–582.

23. Bonilla, P., Dvorak, J., Mackill, D. et al. (2002). RFLP and SSLP mapping of salinity tolerance genes in chromosome 1 of rice (Oryza sativa L.) using recombinant inbred lines. Philipp Agric. Sci. 85: 68–76.

24. Breseghello, F. and Guedes, A.S. (2013). Traditional and modern plant breeding methods with examples in rice (Oryza sativa L.). J. Agric. Food Chem. 35: 8277–8286.

25. Carroll, D. (2014). Genome engineering with targetable nucleases. Annu. Rev. Biochem. 83: 409–439.

26. Chapagain, S., Park, Y.C., Kim, J.H., and Jang, C.S. (2018). Oryza sativa salt induced RING E3 ligase 2 (OsSIRP2) acts as a positive regulator of transketolase in plant response to salinity and osmotic stress. Planta 247: 925–939.

27. Cha-um, S., Srianan, B., Pichakum, A., and Kirdmanee, C. (2009). An efficient procedure for embryogenetic callus induction and double haploid plant regeneration through

anther culture of Thai aromatic rice (Oryza sativa L. subsp. indica). In Vitro Cell. Dev. Biol. 45: 171–179.

28. Chen, R., Cheng, Y., Han, S. et al. (2017). Whole genome sequencing and comparative transcriptome analysis of a novel seawater adapted, salt resistant rice cultivar - sea rice 86. BMC Genomics 18: 655.

29. Chinnusamy, V., Jagendorf, A., and Zhu, J.K. (2005). Understanding and improving salt tolerance in plants. Crop Sci. 45: 437–445.

30. Choudhary, M., Wani, S.H., Kumar, P. et al. (2019). QTLian breeding for climate resilience in cereals: progress and prospects. Funct. Integr. Genomics 19: 685–701.

31. Chutimanukul, P., Kositsup, B., Plaimas, K. et al. (2018). Photosynthetic responses and identification of salt tolerance genes in a chromosome segment substitution line of "Khao Dawk Mali 105" rice. Environ. Exp. Bot. 155: 497–508.

32. Cohen-Tannoudji, M., Robine, S., Choulika, A. et al. (1998). I-SceI-induced gene replacement at a natural locus in embryonic stem cells. Mol. Cell. Biol. 18: 1444–1448.

33. Colaco, A.F., Molin, J.S., Rossel-polo, J.R., and Escola, A. (2018). Application of light detection and ranging and ultrasonic sensors to high-throughput phenotyping and precision horticulture: current status and challenges. Hortic. Res. 1: 1.

34. Collins, N.C., Tardieu, F., and Tuberosa, R. (2008). Quantitative trait loci and crop performance under abiotic stress: where do we stand? Plant Physiol. 147: 469–486.

35. Cong, L., Ran, F.A., Cox, D. et al. (2013). Multiplex genome engineering using CRISPR/Cas systems. Science 339: 819–823.

36. Cui, Y.R., Zhang, F., and Zhou, Y.L. (2018). The application of multi-locus GWAS for the detection of salt-tolerance loci in rice. Front. Plant Sci. 9: 1464.

37. Das, P., Mishra, M., Lakra, N. et al. (2014). Mutation breeding: a powerful approach for obtaining abiotic stress tolerant crops and upgrading food security for human nutrition. In: Mutagenesis: Exploring Novel Genes and Pathways (eds. N.B. Tomlekova, M.I. Kozgar and M.R. Wani), 15–36.

38. De Leon, T.B., Linscombe, S., and Subudhi, P.K. (2016). Molecular dissection of seedling salinity tolerance in rice (Oryza sativa L.) using a high-density GBS-based SNP linkage map. Rice 9: 52.

39. De Leon, T.B., Linscombe, S., and Subudhi, P.K. (2017). Identification and validation of QTLs for seedling salinity tolerance in introgression lines of a salt tolerant rice landrace "Pokkali.". PLoS ONE 12: e0175361.

40. De Leon, T.B., Linscombe, S., Gregorio, G.B., and Subudhi, P.K. (2015). Genetic variation in Southern USA rice genotypes for seedling salinity tolerance. Front. Plant Sci. 6: 374.

41. Deng, P., Jiang, D., Dong, Y. et al. (2015). Physiological characterization and fine mapping of salt-tolerant mutant in rice (Oryza sativa). Funct. Plant Biol. 42: 1026–1035.

42. Dou, M., Fan, S., Yang, S. et al. (2017). Overexpression of AmRosea1 gene confers drought and salt tolerance in rice. Int. J. Mol. Sci. 18: 2.

43. Duan, Y.B., Li, J., Qin, R.Y. et al. (2016). Identification of a regulatory element responsible for salt induction of rice OSRAV2 through ex situ and in situ promoter analysis. Plant Mol. Biol. 90: 49–62.

44. Elshire, R.J., Glaubitz, J.C., Poland, J.A. et al. (2011). A robust, simple genotyping-bysequencing (GBS) approach for high diversity species. PLoS ONE 6: 1–10.

45. Fan, H., Zhang, J., Liu, X. et al. (2016). Effect of different potassium levels on the growth and photosynthesis of sweet sorghum seedlings under salinity stress. In: Proc. Intl. Conf. on Energy, Environmental, and Material Science (EEMS 2015). Guanghzou, China, August 25-26, 2015, pp 169–173.

46. FAO (2008). FAO Land and Plant Nutrition Management Service. http://www.fao.org/ag/agl/ agll/spush

47. Fita, A., Rodríguez-Burruezo, A., Boscaiu, M. et al. (2015). Breeding and domesticating crops adapted to drought and salinity: a new paradigm for increasing food production. Front. Plant Sci. 6: 978.

48. Formentin, E., Sudiro, C., Perin, G. et al. (2018). Transcriptome and cell physiological analyses in different rice cultivars provide new insights into adaptive and salinity stress response. Front. Plant. Sci. 9: 204.

49. Fotoukian, M.H., Taleei, A.R., Gharahyazi, B. et al. (2005). QTL mapping of genes affecting salt tolerance in rice (Oryza sativa L.) using microsatellite markers. Iran. J. Crop. Sci. 6: 361–373.

50. Frouin, J., Languillaume, A., Mas, J. et al. (2018). Tolerance to mild salinity stress in japonica rice: a genome-wide association mapping study highlights calcium signaling and metabolism genes. PLoS ONE 13: e0190964.

51. Ganie, S.A., Pani, D.R., and Mondal, T.K. (2017). Genome-wide analysis of DUF221 domain-containing gene family in Oryza species and identification of its salinity stress-responsive members in rice. PLoS ONE 12: e0182469.

52. Gehan, M.A., Fahlgren, N., Abbasi, A. et al. (2017). PlantCV v2: image analysis software for high-throghput plant phenotyping. Peer J. 5: e4088.

53. Germana, M.A. (2011). Gametic embryogenesis and haploid technology as valuable support to plant breeding. Plant Cell Rep. 30: 839–857.

54. Gimhani, D.R., Gregorio, G.B., and Kottearachchi, N.S. (2016). SNP-based discovery of salinity-tolerant QTLs in a bi-parental population of rice (Oryza sativa). Mol. Genet. Genomics 291: 2081–2099.

55. Gong, J., He, P., Qian, Q. et al. (1999). Identification of salt-tolerance QTL in rice (Oryza sativa L.). Chin. Sci. Bull. 44: 68–71.

56. Gregorio, G.B., Senadhira, D., Mendoza, R.D. et al. (2002). Progress in breeding for salinity tolerance and associated abiotic stresses in rice. Field Crops Res. 76: 91–101.

57. Grenier, C., Cao, T.-V., Ospina, Y. et al. (2015). Accuracy of genomic selection in a rice synthetic population developed for recurrent selection breeding. PLoS ONE 11: e0154976

58. Guo, Q., Wu, F., Pang, S. et al. (2018). Crop 3D—a LiDAR based platform for 3D high-throughput crop phenotyping. Sci. China-Life Sci. 61: 328–339.

59. Karan, R. and Subudhi, P.K. (2011). Approaches to increasing salt tolerance in crop plants. In: Abiotic Stress Responses in Plants: Metabolism to Productivity (eds. P. Ahmad and M.N.V. Prasad), 63–88. New York: Springer Science+Business Media. Springer.

60. Kathuria, H., Giri, J., Tyagi, H., and Tyagi, A. (2007). Advances in transgenic rice biotechnology. Crit. Rev. Plant Sci. 26: 65–103.

61. Kim, D.M., Ju, H.G., Kwon, T.R. et al. (2009). Mapping QTLs for salt tolerance in an introgression lines population between japonica cultivars in rice. J. Crop. Sci. Biotech. 12: 121–128.

62. Kim, S.L., Chung, Y.S., Silva, R.R. et al. (2019). The opening of phenome-assisted selection era in the early seedling stage. Sci. Rep. 1: 1.

63. Klose, R., Penlington, J., and Ruckelshausen, A. (2009). Usability study of 3D time-of-flight cameras for automatic plant phenotyping. BornimerAgrartech. 69: 93–105.

64. Kumar, K., Kumar, M., Kim, S.R. et al. (2013). Insights into genomics of salt stress responses in rice. Rice 6: 27.

65. Kumar, M., Choi, J., An, G., and Kim, S.R. (2017). Ectopic expression of OsSta2 enhances salt stress tolerance in rice. Front. Plant Sci. 8: 316.

66. Kumar, V., Singh, A., Mithra, S.V.A. et al. (2015). Genome-wide association mapping of salinity tolerance in rice (Oryza sativa). DNA Res. 22: 133–145.

67. Lang, N.T., Buu, B.C., and Ismai, A. (2008). Molecular mapping and marker-assisted selection for salt tolerance in rice (Oryza sativa L.). Omon Rice 16: 50–56.

68. Lee, I.S., Kim, D.S., Hyun, D.Y. et al. (2003a). Isolation of gamma-induced rice mutants with increased tolerance to salt by anther culture. J. Plant Biotech. 5: 51–57.

69. Lee, K.S., Choi, W.Y., Ko, J.C. et al. (2003b). Salinity tolerance of japonica and indica rice (Oryza sativa L.) at the seedling stage. Planta 216: 1043–1046.

70. Lekklar, C., Pongpanich, M., Suriya-arunroj, D. et al. (2019). Genome-wide association study for salinity tolerance at the flowering stage in a panel of rice accessions from Thailand. BMC Genom. 20: 76.

71. Li, L., Zhang, Q., and Huang, D. (2014). A review of imaging techniques for plant phenotyping. Sensors (Basel) 11: 20078.

72. Li, W., Qiang, X.J., Han, X.R. et al. (2018). Ectopic expression of a Thellungiellasalsuginea aquaporin gene, TsPIP1;1, increased the salt tolerance of rice. Int. J. Mol. Sci. 19: 2229.

73. Liao, Y.D., Lin, K.H., Chen, C.C., and Chang, C.M. (2016). Oryza sativa protein phosphatase 1a (OsPP1a) involved in salt stress tolerance in transgenic rice. Mol. Breed. 36: 22.

74. Lim, S.D., Jung, C.G., Park, Y.C. et al. (2015). Molecular dissection of a rice microtubule-associated RING finger protein and its potential role in salt tolerance in Arabidopsis. Mol. Biol. 89: 365–384.

75. Lin, H.X., Zhu, M.Z., Yano, M. et al. (2004). QTLs for Na^+ and K^+ uptake of the shoots and roots controlling rice salt tolerance. Theor. Appl. Gnet. 108: 253–260.

76. Linh, H.L., Linh, H.T., Xuan, D.T. et al. (2012). Molecular breeding to improve salt tolerance of rice (Oryza sativa L.) in the red river delta of Vietnam. Int. J. Plant Genomics. 2012: 949038. https://doi.org/10.1155/2012/949038.

77. Mansuri, R.M., Shobbar, Z.S., Jelodar, N.B. et al. (2019). Dissecting molecular mechanisms underlying salt tolerance in rice: a comparative transcriptional profiling of the contrasting genotypes. Rice 1: 1.

78. Masood, M.S., Seiji, Y., Shinwari, Z.K., and Anwar, R. (2004). Mapping quantitative trait loci (QTLs) for salt tolerance in rice (Oryza sativa L.). using RFLPs. Pak. J. Bot. 36: 825–834.

79. McCouch, S.R. and Kovach, M.J. (2008). Leveraging natural diversity: back through the bottleneck. Curr. Opin. Plant Biol. 11: 193–200.

80. Mir, R.R., Reynolds, M., Pinto, F. et al. (2019). High-throughput phenotyping for crop improvement in the genomics era. Plant Sci. 282: 60–72.

81. Mishra, B. (1994). Breeding for salt tolerance in crops. In: Salinity Management for Sustainable Agriculture (eds. D.L.N. Rao, N.T. Singh, R.K. Gupta and N.K. Tyagi), 226–259. Karnal, India: Central Soil Salinity Research Institute.

82. Mishra, S., Singh, B., Misra, P. et al. (2016). Haplotype distribution and association of candidate genes with salt tolerance in Indian wild rice germplasm. Plant Cell Rep. 35: 2295–2308.

83. Mohammadi, R., Mendioro, M.S., Diaz, G.Q. et al. (2013). Mapping quantitative trait loci associated with yield and yield components under reproductive stage salinity stress in rice (Oryza sativa L.). J. Genet. 92: 433–443.

84. Munns, R. (2002). Comparative physiology of salt and water stress. Plant Cell Environ. 25: 239–250. Munns, R. (2005). Genes and salt tolerance: bringing them together. New Phytol. 167: 645–663.

85. Munns, R. and Gilliham, M. (2015). Salinity tolerance of crops—what is the cost? New Phytol. 208: 668–673.

86. Munns, R. and Tester, M. (2008). Mechanisms of salinity tolerance. Annu. Rev. Plant Biol. 59: 651–681.

87. Munns, R., James, R.A., and Läuchli, A. (2006). Approaches to increasing the salt tolerance of wheat and other cereals. J. Exp. Bot. 57: 1025–1043.

88. Munns, R., James, R.A., Furbank, R.T. et al. (2010). New phenotyping methods for screening wheat and barley for beneficial responses to water deficit. J. Exp. Bot. 61: 3499–3507.

89. Mustafa, G., Soomro, A.M., Baloch, A.W., and Siddiqui, K.A. (1997). "Shua-92," a new cultivar of rice (Oryza sativa L) developed through fast neutrons irradiation. Mutation Breeding Newsletter, IAEA, Vienna, Austria, 43: 35–36.

90. Naveed, S.A., Zhang, F., Zhang, J. et al. (2018). Identification of QTN and candidate genes for salinity tolerance at the germination and seedling stages in rice by genome-wide association analyses. Sci. Rep. 8: 6505.

91. Negrão, S., Almadanim, M.C., Pires, I.S. et al. (2013). New allelic variants found in key rice salt-tolerance genes: an association study. Plant Biotechnol. J. 11: 87–100.

92. Negrão, S., Courtois, B., Ahmadi, N. et al. (2011). Recent updates on salinity stress in rice: from physiological to molecular responses. Crit. Rev. Plant Sci. 30: 329–377.

93. Nounjan, N., Siangliw, J.L., Toojinda, T. et al. (2016). Salt-responsive mechanisms in chromosome segment substitution lines of rice (Oryza sativa L. cv. KDML105). Plant Physiol. Biochem. 103: 96–105.

94. Oono, Y., Kawahara, Y., Kanamori, H. et al. (2011). mRNA-Seq reveals a comprehensive transcriptome profile of rice under phosphate stress. Rice 4: 50–65

95. *Plant Abiotic Stress Tolerance* (eds. N. Tuteja, S.S. Gill and R. Tuteja), 10–38. Bentham Science Publishers Ltd. https://doi.org/10.2174/97816080505811110101.

96. Platten, J.D., Egdane, J.A., and Ismail, A.M. (2013). Salinity tolerance, Na^+ exclusion and allele mining of *HKT1;5* in *Oryza sativa* and *O. glaberrima*: many sources, many genes, one mechanism? *BMC Plant Biol.* 13: 32.

97. Prasad, S.R., Bagali, P.G., Hittalmani, S., & Shashidhar, H.E. (2000). Molecular mapping of quantitative trait loci associated with seedling tolerance to salt stress in rice (*Oryza sativa* L.). *Current Science, 78*, 162-164.

98. Prusty, M. R., Kim, S. R., Vinarao, R., Entila, F., Egdane, J., Diaz, M. G. Q., & Jena, K. K. (2018). Newly Identified Wild Rice Accessions Conferring High Salt Tolerance Might Use a Tissue Tolerance Mechanism in Leaf. *Frontiers in plant science, 9*, 417. https://doi.org/10.3389/fpls.2018.00417

99. Punyawaew, K., Suriya-arunroj, D., Siangliw, M., Thida, M., Lanceras-Siangliw, J., Fukai, S., & Toojinda, T. (2016). Thai jasmine rice cultivar KDML105 carrying Saltol QTL exhibiting salinity tolerance at seedling stage. *Molecular Breeding, 36*, 1-13.

100. Puram, V.R.R., Ontoy, J., and Subudhi, P.K. (2018). Identification of QTLs for salt tolerance traits and prebreeding lines with enhanced salt tolerance in an introgression line population of rice. *Plant Mol. Biol. Rep.* 36: 695–709.

101. Puram, V.R.R., Ontoy, J., Linscombe, S., and Subudhi, P.K. (2017). Genetic dissection of seedling stage salinity tolerance in rice using introgression lines of a salt tolerant landrace Nona Bokra. *J. Hered.* 108: 658–670.

102. Quijano-Guerta, C. and Kirk, G.J.D. (2002). Tolerance of rice germplasm to salinity and other soil chemical stresses in tidal wetlands. *Field Crops Res.* 76: 111–121.

103. Rahman, H., Ramanathan, V., Nallathambi, J. et al. (2016). Over-expression of a NAC 67 transcription factor from finger millet (*Eleusine coracana* L.) confers tolerance against salinity and drought stress in rice. *BMC Biotechnol.* 16 (Suppl 1): 35.

104. Rahman, M.A., Bimpong, I.K., Bizimana, J.B. et al. (2017). Mapping QTLs using a novel source of salinity tolerance from Hasawi and their interaction with environments in rice. *Rice* 10: 47.

105. Rajendran, K., Tester, M., and Roy, S.J. (2009). Quantifying the three main components of salinity tolerance in cereals. *Plant Cell Environ.* 32: 237–249.

106. Rana, M. M., Takamatsu, T., Baslam, M., Kaneko, K., Itoh, K., Harada, N., Sugiyama, T., Ohnishi, T., Kinoshita, T., Takagi, H., & Mitsui, T. (2019). Salt Tolerance Improvement in Rice through Efficient SNP Marker-Assisted Selection Coupled with Speed-Breeding. *International journal of molecular sciences, 20*(10), 2585. https://doi.org/10.3390/ijms20102585

107. Rashid, M.H. and Nasrin, S. (2015). Productivity and preference of salt tolerant Boro rice varieties in saline non-gher and gher ecosystems. *Bangladesh Rice J.* 18 (1–2): 18–23.

108. Reddy, A.M., Francies, R.M., Rasool, S.N., and Reddy, V.R.P. (2014). Breeding for tolerance stress triggered by salinity in rice. *Int. J. Appl. Biol. Pharm.* 5: 167–176.

109. Reddy, I.N.B.L., Kim, B.K., In-Sun Yoon, I.S., and Kim, K.H. (2017). Salt tolerance in rice: focus on mechanisms and approaches. *Rice Sci.* 24: 123–144.

110. Ren, Z., Gao, J., Li, L. et al. (2005). A rice quantitative trait locus for salt tolerance encodes a sodium transporter. *Nat. Genet.* 37: 1141–1146.

111. Robertsen, C.D., Rasmus, L., Hjortshøj, R.L., and Janss, L.L. (2019). Genomic selection in cereal breeding. *Agronomy* 9: 95.

112. Roy, S. J., Negrão, S., & Tester, M. (2014). Salt resistant crop plants. *Current opinion in biotechnology, 26*, 115–124. https://doi.org/10.1016/j.copbio.2013.12.004

113. Sabouri, H. and Sabouri, A. (2008). New evidence of QTLs attributed to salinity tolerance in rice. *Afr. J. Biotechnol.* 7: 4376–4383.

114. Sakina, A., Ahmed, I., Shahzad, A. et al. (2016). Genetic variation for salinity tolerance in Pakistani rice (*Oryza sativa* L.) germplasm. *J. Agron. Crop. Sci.* 202: 25–36.

115. Saleem, M.Y., Mukhtar, Z., Cheema, A.A., and Atta, B.M. (2005). Induced mutation and in vitro techniques as a method to induce salt tolerance in Basmati rice (*Oryza sativa* L.). *Int. J. Environ. Sci. Technol.* 2: 141–145.

116. Samaco, Manuela & Villa, Neilyn & Gregorio, Glenn. (2018). Salinity tolerance and traits correlations of selected magic indica rice (Oryza sativa L.) genotypes at seedling stage. Philippine Agricultural Scientist. 101. 312-325.

117. Sengupta, S. and Majumder, A.L. (2010). *Porteresiacoarctata* (Roxb.) Tateoka, a wild rice: a potential model for studying salt-stress biology in rice. *Plant Cell Environ.* 33: 526–542.

118. Shahbaz, Muhammad & Ashraf, Muhammad. (2013). Improving Salinity Tolerance in Cereals. Critical Reviews in Plant Sciences. 32. 10.1080/07352689.2013.758544.

119. Shankar, R., Bhattacharjee, A., & Jain, M. (2016). Transcriptome analysis in different rice cultivars provides novel insights into desiccation and salinity stress responses. *Scientific reports, 6,* 23719. https://doi.org/10.1038/srep23719

120. Shelden, M.C. and Roessner, U. (2013). Advances in functional genomics for investigating salinity stress tolerance mechanisms in cereals. *Front. Plant Sci.* 4: 123.

121. Shi, Y., Gao, L., Wu, Z. et al. (2017). Genome-wide association study of salt tolerance at the seed germination stage in rice. *BMC Plant Biol.* 17: 92.

122. Singh, B., Mishra, S., Bohra, A. et al. (2018a). Crop phenomics for abiotic stress tolerance in crop plants. In: *Biochemical, Physiological and Molecular Avenues for Combating Abiotic Stress Tolerance in Plants* (ed. S.H. Wani), 277–296. New York: Elsevier.

123. Singh, N., Choudhury, D.R., Tiwari, G. et al. (2016a). Genetic diversity trend in Indian rice variety: an analysis using SSR markers. *BMC Genet.* 17: 1–13.

124. Singh, R., Singh, Y., Xalaxo, Y. et al. (2016b). From QTL to variety-harnessing the benefits of QTLs for drought, flood and salt tolerance in mega rice varieties of India through a multi-institutional network. *Plant Sci.* 242: 278–287.

125. Singh, R.K., Gopalakrishnan, S., Singh, V.P. et al. (2011). Marker assisted selection: a paradigm shift in basmati breeding. *Indian J. Genet.* 71: 120–128.

126. Singh, V. K., Singh, B. D., Kumar, A., Maurya, S., Krishnan, S. G., Vinod, K. K., Singh, M. P., Ellur, R. K., Bhowmick, P. K., & Singh, A. K. (2018). Marker-Assisted Introgression of *Saltol* QTL Enhances Seedling Stage Salt Tolerance in the Rice Variety "Pusa Basmati 1". *International journal of genomics, 2018,* 8319879. https://doi.org/10.1155/2018/8319879

127. Spindel, J. and Iwata, H. (2018). Genomic selection in rice breeding. In: *Rice Genomics, Genetics and Breeding* (eds. T. Sasaki and M. Ashikari), 473–496.

128. Subudhi PK, Baisakh N (2011) *Spartina alterniflora* Loisel., a halophyte grass model to dissect salt stress tolerance. In Vitro Cell Dev Biol – Plant 47:441-457.

129. Takagi, H., Abe, A., Yoshida, K., Kosugi, S., Natsume, S., Mitsuoka, C., Uemura, A., Utsushi, H., Tamiru, M., Takuno, S., Innan, H., Cano, L. M., Kamoun, S., & Terauchi, R. (2013). QTL-seq: rapid mapping of quantitative trait loci in rice by whole genome resequencing of DNA from two bulked populations. *The Plant journal: for cell and molecular biology, 74*(1), 174–183. https://doi.org/10.1111/tpj.12105

130. Takagi, H., Tamiru, M., Abe, A. et al. (2015). MutMap accelerates breeding of a salt-tolerant rice cultivar. *Nat. Biotechnol.* 33: 445–449.

131. Takehisa, H., Shimodate, T., Fukuta, Y. et al. (2004). Identification of quantitative trait loci for plant growth of rice in paddy field flooded with salt water. *Field Crops Res.* 89: 85–95.

132. Tamimi, N.A., Brien, C., Oakey, H. et al. (2016). Salinity tolerance loci revealed in rice using high-throughput non-invasive phenotyping. *Nat. Commun.* 7: 13342.

133. Tang, Y., Bao, X., Zhi, Y. et al. (2019). Overexpression of a MYB family gene, *OsMYB6*, increases drought and salinity stress tolerance in transgenic rice. *Front. Plant Sci.* 10: 168.

134. Thitisaksakul, M., Tananuwong, K., Shoemaker, C. F., Chun, A., Tanadul, O. U., Labavitch, J. M., & Beckles, D. M. (2015). Effects of timing and severity of salinity stress on rice (*Oryza sativa* L.) yield, grain composition, and starch functionality. *Journal of agricultural and food chemistry, 63*(8), 2296–2304. https://doi.org/10.1021/jf503948p

135. Thomson, M.J., Ocampo, M., and Egdane, J. (2010). Characterizing the *Saltol*quantitative trait locus for salinity tolerance in rice. *Rice* 3: 148–160.

136. Thuy, N.T., Tokuyasu, M., Mai, N.T., and Hirai, Y. (2018). Identification and characterization of chromosome regions associated with salinity tolerance in rice. *J. Agric. Sci.* 10 (11): 57–68. https://doi.org/10.5539/jas.v10n11p57.

137. Tiwari, S., Krishnamurthy, S.L., Kumar, V. et al. (2016). Mapping of QTLs for salt tolerance in rice (*Oryza sativa* L.) by bulked segregant analysis of recombinant inbred lines using 50K SNP chip. *PLoS ONE* 11: e0153610.

138. Tsai, Y.C., Chen, K.C., Cheng, T.S. et al. (2019). Chlorophyll fluorecence analysis in diverse rice varieties reveals the positive correaltion between the seedlings' salt tolerance and photosynthetic efficiency. *BMC Plant Biol.* 19: 403.

139. Valarmathi, M., Sasikala, R.P., Rahman, H., Jagadeeshselvam, N., Kambale, R., & Raveendran, M. (2019). Development of salinity tolerant version of a popular rice

variety improved white ponni through marker assisted back cross breeding. *Indian Journal of Plant Physiology*, 1-10.

140. Van As, H., Scheenen, T., and Vergeldt, F.J. (2009). MRI of intact plants. *Photosynth. Res.* 102:

141. Vu, H.T.T., Le, D.D., Ismail, A.M., and Le, H.H. (2012). Marker-assisted backcrossing (MABC) for improved salinity tolerance in rice (*Oryza sativa* L.). to cope with climate change in Vietnam. *Aust. J. Crop Sci.* 6: 1649–1654.

142. Wageningen: Wageningen Academic Publisher. Das, P., Nutan, K.K., Singla-Pareek, S.L., and Pareek, A. (2015). Understanding salinity responses and adopting "omics-based" approaches to generate salinity tolerant cultivars of rice. *Front. Plant Sci.* 6: 712.

143. Wang, B., Zhong, Z., Zhang, H. et al. (2019). Targeted mutagenesis of NAC transcription factor gene. *OsNAC041,* leading to salt sensitivity in rice. *Rice Sci.* 26: 98–108.

144. Wang, C., Yang, Y., Wang, H. et al. (2016). Ectopic expression of a cytochrome P450 monooxygenase gene PtCYP714A3 from *Populus trichocarpa*reduces shoot growth and improves tolerance to salt stress in transgenic rice. *Plant Biotechnol. J.* 149: 1838–1851.

145. Wang, J., Zhu, J., Zhang, Y. et al. (2017a). Comparative transcriptome analysis reveals molecular responses to salinity stress of salt tolerant and sensitive genotypes of *indica* rice at seedling stage. *Sci. Rep.* 8: 2045–2322.

146. Wang, X., Li, L., Yang, Z. et al. (2017b). Predicting rice hybrid performance using univariate and multivariate GBLUP models based on North Carolina mating design II. *Heredity* 118:

147. Xiang, D.J., Man, L.L., Zhang, C.L. et al. (2018). A new Em-like protein from *Lactuca sativa, LsEm1*, enhances drought and salt stress tolerance in *Escherichia coli* and rice. *Protoplasma*255: 1089–1106.

148. Yu, J., Zhao, W., He, Q. et al. (2017). Genome-wide association study and gene set analysis for understanding candidate genes involved in salt tolerance at the rice seedling stage. *Mol. Genet. Genomics* 292: 1391–1403.

149. Yu, J., Zhao, W., Tong, W. et al. (2018). A genome-wide association study reveals candidate genes related to salt tolerance in rice (*Oryza sativa*) at the germination stage. *Int. J. Mol. Sci.* 19: 3145.

150. Zang, J.P., Sun, Y., Wang, Y. et al. (2008). Dissection of genetic overlap of salt tolerance QTLs at the seedling and tillering stages using backcross introgression lines in rice. *Sci. China C Life Sci.* 51: 583–591.

151. Zeng, L. and Shannon, M.C. (2000). Salinity effects on seedling growth and yield components of rice. *Crop. Sci.* 40: 996–100.

152. Zhang, A., Liu, Y., Wang, F. et al. (2019). Enhanced rice salinity tolerance via CRISPR/Cas9-targeted mutagenesis of the *OsRR22* gene. *Mol. Breed.* 39: 47.

153. Zhang, D., Wang, Z., Wang, N. et al. (2014). Tissue culture-induced heritable genomic variations in rice, and their phenotypic implications. *PLoS ONE* 9: 1–10.

154. Zhang, Y., Fang, J., Wu, X., and Dong, L. (2018). Na^+/K^+ balance and transport regulatory mechanisms in weedy and cultivated rice (*Oryza sativa* L.) under salt stress. *BMC Plant Biol.* 18: 375.

155. Zhou, Y., Liu, C., Tang, D. et al. (2018). The receptor-like cytoplasmic kinase STRK1 phosphorylates and activates CatC, thereby regulating H_2O_2 homeostasis and improving salt tolerance in rice. *Plant Cell* 30 (5): 1100–1118. https://doi.org/10.1105/tpc.17.01000.